The Refugee Aesthetic

In the series *Asian American History and Culture,*
edited by Cathy Schlund-Vials, Shelley Sang-Hee Lee, and Rick Bonus.
Founding editor, Sucheng Chan; editors emeriti, David Palumbo-Liu,
Michael Omi, K. Scott Wong, and Linda Trinh Võ.

Also in this series:

Heidi Kim, *Illegal Immigrants/Model Minorities: The Cold War of Chinese American Narrative* (forthcoming)
Chia Youyee Vang with Pao Yang, Retired Captain, U.S. Secret War in Laos, *Prisoner of Wars: A Hmong Fighter Pilot's Story of Escaping Death and Confronting Life* (forthcoming)
Kavita Daiya, *Graphic Migrations: Precarity and Gender in India and the Diaspora* (forthcoming)
L. Joyce Zapanta Mariano, *Giving Back: Filipino Diaspora and the Politics of Giving* (forthcoming)
Manan Desai, *The United States of India: Anticolonial Literature and Transnational Refraction*
Cathy J. Schlund-Vials, Guy Beauregard, and Hsiu-chuan Lee, eds., *The Subject(s) of Human Rights: Crises, Violations, and Asian/American Critique*
Malini Johar Schueller, *Campaigns of Knowledge: U.S. Pedagogies of Colonialism and Occupation in the Philippines and Japan*
Crystal Mun-hye Baik, *Reencounters: On the Korean War and Diasporic Memory Critique*
Michael Omi, Dana Y. Nakano, and Jeffrey T. Yamashita, eds., *Japanese American Millennials: Rethinking Generation, Community, and Diversity*
Masumi Izumi, *The Rise and Fall of America's Concentration Camp Law: Civil Liberties Debates from the Internment to McCarthyism and the Radical 1960s*
Shirley Jennifer Lim, *Anna May Wong: Performing the Modern*
Edward Tang, *From Confinement to Containment: Japanese/American Arts during the Early Cold War*
Patricia P. Chu, *Where I Have Never Been: Migration, Melancholia, and Memory in Asian American Narratives of Return*
Cynthia Wu, *Sticky Rice: A Politics of Intraracial Desire*
Marguerite Nguyen, *America's Vietnam: The Longue Durée of U.S. Literature and Empire*
Vanita Reddy, *Fashioning Diaspora: Beauty, Femininity, and South Asian American Culture*

A list of additional titles in this series appears at the back of this book.

Timothy K. August

The Refugee Aesthetic

REIMAGINING SOUTHEAST ASIAN AMERICA

TEMPLE UNIVERSITY PRESS   *Philadelphia • Rome • Tokyo*

TEMPLE UNIVERSITY PRESS
Philadelphia, Pennsylvania 19122
tupress.temple.edu

Copyright © 2021 by Temple University—Of The Commonwealth System
 of Higher Education
All rights reserved
Published 2021

Library of Congress Cataloging-in-Publication Data

Names: August, Timothy K., 1979– author.
Title: The refugee aesthetic : reimagining Southeast Asian America /
 Timothy K. August.
Other titles: Asian American history and culture.
Description: Philadelphia : Temple University Press, 2021. | Series: Asian
 American history and culture | Includes bibliographical references and
 index. | Summary: "Effectively synthesizes current theoretical
 discussions of refugee cultural interventions and Asian American
 aesthetics and uses a literary and artistic focus to ask how refugees
 and refuge have been represented and imagined over the last century.
 Intervenes with a "refugee aesthetic" analytic that rethinks and
 re-empowers refugee positions, perspectives, and experiences"— Provided
 by publisher.
Identifiers: LCCN 2020010577 (print) | LCCN 2020010578 (ebook) |
 ISBN 9781439915301 (cloth) | ISBN 9781439915318 (paperback) |
 ISBN 9781439915325 (pdf)
Subjects: LCSH: Southeast Asian Americans—Ethnic identity. | Refugees
 in literature. | Refugees in art.
Classification: LCC E184.S695 A94 2021 (print) | LCC E184.S695 (ebook) |
 DDC 305.895/073—dc23
LC record available at https://lccn.loc.gov/2020010577
LC ebook record available at https://lccn.loc.gov/2020010578

9 8 7 6 5 4 3 2 1

For my parents

Contents

Acknowledgments ix

Refugee Aesthetics: An Introduction 1

1 The Refugee Image 25

2 The Refugee Position 55

3 Refugee Space 78

4 The Refugee Personality 98

Refugee Futures: A Conclusion 124

Notes 133
Bibliography 149
Index 159

Acknowledgments

I owe an enormous debt to the various refugee artists and authors who appear throughout this book for their inspiration, courage, and willingness to allow me to use their material. And indeed, I want to acknowledge up front that this book is built off the backs of many artists, authors, and academics of color, and to be able to access the creative artwork, forms of mentorship, and resources necessary to write this book is a privilege that I do not take lightly.

I am also indebted to my editors, Sara Jo Cohen, Sarah Munroe, and Aaron Javsicas, and the entire staff at Temple University Press. Their help at various stages of the publication process has made this collaboration enjoyable and rewarding. I would also like to thank the two reviewers of the book whose astute suggestions elevated and enhanced this project. Select portions of this book have appeared in different forms. Chapter 4 is a revision of "Spies Like Us: A Professor Undercover in the Literary Marketplace," *LIT: Literature Interpretation Theory* 29.1 (2018): 60–79, DOI: 10.1080/10436928.2018.1416252, which can be found in a special issue edited by Cathy Schlund-Vials. Chapter 2 builds from "Re-placing the Accent: From the Exile to Refugee Position," *MELUS: Multi-Ethnic Literature of the United States* 41.3

(2016): 68–88, which forms part of a special issue edited by Marguerite Nguyen and Catherine Fung. I extend my thanks to Taylor & Francis (https://www.tandfonline.com/) and Oxford University Press for their permission to use these materials.

This work could not have been completed without the help of Stony Brook University's FAHSS Award, President's Distinguished Travel Award, and the AHLSS Faculty Research Program Award. I also benefited from numerous Individual Development Awards offered by our union, the United University Professions. I am immensely grateful to the Southeast Asian Archive at the University of California, Irvine, for the Anne Frank Visiting Researcher Award. I would like to thank Thuy Vo Dang in particular for her continuing expertise in researching, finding, scanning, and tracking down permissions for images used in this book. I am also grateful to Mariam Durrani, James Kim, Yvonne Kwan, Yuich Onishi, and Jinyoung Jin for inviting me to speak at events that helped forge many of the ideas found in the book and to Jinyoung and Sina Kim for allowing me to use a picture of the installation they created in Stony Brook's Wang Center for the cover image of this book.

It gives me great pleasure to express my appreciation for the teachers, colleagues, and friends who helped me in different ways so I could write this book. Early on in my halcyon and unformed days, I benefited greatly from the classes and mentorship offered by Eric Cazdyn and Sam Solecki at the University of Toronto, who showed me worlds that existed outside my home and native land of Scarborough. Lily Cho and Michael Gardiner introduced me to what it means to be an academic while I was at the University of Western Ontario, and importantly, Lily modeled for me the type of person I continue to strive to be as I move through this profession. At the University of Minnesota I was brought through the Ph.D. process by the reliable guidance and intellectual rigor of Keya Ganguly, learning immensely from her, as well as Josephine Lee, Timothy Brennan, Donna Gabaccia, Jeffrey Pilcher, Erika Lee, Shaden Tageldin, and Robin Brown. The opportunity to work at *Cultural Critique* educated me about the publishing process and was an invaluable apprenticeship. No one has taught me more about writing than Katie Levin, and the short time I spent at the Center for Writing was one of the most indispensable experiences of my career. In addition, at Minnesota I benefited greatly from being challenged and nurtured by an excellent cohort of friends and colleagues such as Garnet Kindervater, Sara Saljoughi, Namrata Gaikwad, Elizabeth Zanoni, Tom Sarmiento, Juliana Hu Pegues, and Stephen Suh. I have been very fortunate to have received incredible support from faculty, staff, and friends here at Stony Brook, led by Celia Marshik, Mary Jo Bona, Iona Man Cheong, Jeff Santa Ana, Nerissa Balce, Shirley Lim, Nancy Hiemstra, Liz Montegary, Mike Rubenstein, Lisa Diedrich, Robert Harvey, Sue Bottigheimer, Amy Cook, Ken Weitzman, Mary Moran-Luba, Theresa Spadola, Margaret Hanley, Jacob Gaboury, Simoni Brioni, and Nikos Panou. E. K. Tan has been a particularly vibrant force and mentor throughout my time here, sustaining me, always, with his generosity, intelligence, care, and wit.

The Association for Asian American Studies has been a second home to me, and I am eternally grateful for all the support I have received from friends such as Catherine Nguyen, Vinh Nguyen, Evyn Lê Espiritu Gandhi, Jason Oliver Chang, Nina Ha, Mark Padoongpatt, Caroline Kyungah Hong, Mai-Linh Hong, Việt Lê, Aline Lo, Chris Eng, and Ivan Small as well as the moral and practical backing I have received from more senior colleagues such as erin Khue Ninh, Martin Manalansan, Robert Ji-Song Ku, Viet Thanh Nguyen, Sarah Park Dahlen, Cindy Wu, Martha Cutter, Tina Chen, and Min Hyoung Song. I would also like to extend special mention to faculty who have informally mentored me at various moments in my career, generously offering their time during conferences and travels, namely Linda Trinh Võ, Christopher Lee, Timothy Yu, Leilani Nishime, Mariam Beevi Lam, Sue J. Kim, Isabelle Thuy Pelaud, and Anita Mannur. Finally, I would like to acknowledge two exceptional scholars: Na-Rae Kim, who has been a cherished comrade since our first year in graduate school, where we worked to figure it all out together, and Rei Magosaki, who has been a remarkable mentor and friend, reminding me of both the joys and challenges of professorial life.

Without question, I am particularly indebted to Michele Janette and Cathy Schlund-Vials, for without them my career simply would not exist. They have been unfailing supporters at every turn, providing important corrections and feedback and the courage to push myself to become the academic and person I am today. I only hope that one day I can begin to live up to the examples they have set for me and countless others in our field. However, I am even more indebted to the unfailing and unconditional love and support of my parents, for without them I simply would not exist. I am also indebted to the delights and wonders shown to me by my boys Andrade and Benjamin, who without me simply would not exist. And finally, regarding my dear wife Thien Nguyen August, I am truly thankful and amazed every day that this resourceful, patient, and loving person continues, always, to exist.

The Refugee Aesthetic

Refugee Aesthetics

An Introduction

In a review of Mohsin Hamid's Booker-nominated novel *Exit West* (2017), *The Atlantic*'s Sophie Gilbert offers that Hamid's accomplishment is "not putting a human face on refugees so much as putting a refugee face on all of humankind."[1] Indeed, a major current of *Exit West* is that becoming a refugee could happen to anyone—even to the novel's protagonists, young aspiring professionals in an unnamed city whose lives, at first, do not seem to be much different from the educated and potentially affluent readers of the book. With over twenty-five million refugees worldwide, becoming a refugee is not an exceptional circumstance in the present moment, and the existence of refugees has become an accepted, common, and possibly even distinguishing feature of our contemporary global landscape. Yet for a long time, the experiences of refugees have been reductively cast as unusual and marginal, used to garner support through pity rather than identification with those afflicted with the refugee condition.[2] By contrast, Hamid submits that refugees are, in many ways, just like the readers themselves, too much so perhaps, for if the readers are not careful they could be turned into refugees in the blink of an eye.

It is telling that in Gilbert's formulation there is a distinction made between a "human face" and a "refugee face," as though the refugee face presents something that is other than, or perhaps beyond, the human. Actual faces of refugees have long been of interest to those working in visual media, including journalists, artists, and nonprofit organizations, as they are seen to forge the intimacy necessary to connect the plight of particular refugee people with humanity at large. Refugees are formed through an interconnected global network but are often read by Western audiences as the product of distinct and separate crises, creating a lacuna between universal humanitarian ethics and the political positions of particular refugee groups. This lacuna conceals the interrelated influences of imperialism, neoliberalism, and global capital, most evident recently by the resurgence of nationalistic discourse and interlaced throughout by attending forms of racism. While visual presentations of the refugee experience can bring attention to otherwise underreported global events, relying on sympathy, pity, and emergency focuses attention on the immediate physical attributes and conditions of refugees themselves, which can actively hide the causal linkages between the socioeconomic acts of empire and the production of refugees.[3] In this light, instead of refugees being recognized as structural attributes of global capital accumulation, images of the refugee and the refugee face present viewers with a type of abject experience that is seen as exceptional and best to be avoided altogether.

Of course, the influence that rhetorical patterns have on the reception of refugees is not limited to visual media and can be found in the commonsense usage of refugee narratives, as well. That is, stories about refugee life are seen as effective devices that can provide the details necessary to provoke sympathy, compassion, and action for non-profit agencies and humanitarian endeavors. Chris George of Integrated Refugee & Immigrant Services (IRIS) summarizes the conventional approach to the use of refugee aesthetics by claiming that "when people learn about the IRIS, when they meet refugees and they are humanized through art, they will support the program."[4] While instrumentally this approach allows IRIS to continue its excellent work with and for refugee communities, it is worth considering how and in what ways refugees are expected to be "humanized" through art when they, of course, are always already humans.

The assumption behind this presentation of refugee life, then, is that to most audiences, refugees are in fact not fully human—existing instead as life-forms in transition, dwelling in camps that lay on the edges of nation-states, belonging either to the past or the future but never quite fully inhabiting the present space. IRIS's palatable approach sees art as a way to de-emphasize the differences between the refugees and consumers, presenting refugees as part of a common humanity, but does so at the expense of the complex histories and oppositional politics that refugees can hold and embody. This kind of refugee aesthetic seeks to humanize refugees in ways that counter racially coded political movements that present refugees and other immigrant groups as problematic, damaged, and intrinsically foreign people. But it is worth considering whether these two different rhetorical approaches to refugee life are actually as dichotomous as they first may seem, for both the presentations that evoke sympathy for refugees and the protectionist governmental policies and rhetoric that demonize them seek in the end to eliminate refugees and refugee experience altogether. Instead of actually creating a place for refugees in the present, the hope of "humanizing refugees" is that readers and audiences will drive political transformation to eliminate this condition. However, how does this constant striving to erase the refugee condition place and position those who actually are or are the descendants of refugees? And what does this erasure do to the writing and reception of refugee pasts, presents, and futures? In other words, what imaginative opportunities does one have when writing from the refugee position to a readership that is disturbed by his or her very presence, at least insofar as the writer exists as a refugee?

It is with these questions in mind that I write *The Refugee Aesthetic: Reimagining Southeast Asian America,* a book that in its simplest terms examines how refugees are represented and represent themselves. As the refugee is conventionally considered a powerless figure, eagerly cast aside by both migrant and host communities, this book investigates how and why a number of Southeast Asian American artists have recently embraced the figure of the refugee as a transformative position. In doing so, the book follows how the dominance of a singular refugee aesthetic is currently being challenged by a variety of approaches that recognize the power that refugee aesthetics can hold. This move from a monolithic refugee aesthetic constructed mainly by nonrefugees to a collection of refugee aesthetics fronted by refugees or their descendants is, at the moment, best characterized by narratives that foreground interiority, present multiple refugee subject positions, and reflexively comment upon the ways refugee lives are customarily represented and their expressions received. Reading refugee narratives with a close eye to their form and authorial horizons provides a particular aesthetic analytic that reveals and challenges the overdetermination affecting refugee subjects, both within and beyond the Southeast Asian American example.

The aim of this study, however, is not only to track how a multifarious and flexible refugee aesthetics is challenging the dominance of the singular refugee aesthetic but also to use this emergence to argue that the aesthetic should be a central category in the conceptualization of refugees and refugee thought. Taking no particular type of representation as authentic truth, I instead focus on how refugee aesthetics reveal, produce, and/or dispute the commonalities, disparities, and inequalities that are assumed to exist among refugees and receiving populations. Specifically, *The Refugee Aesthetic* offers four new ways to study this mobile population, as it theorizes the narrative qualities that comprise the refugee aesthetic, generates a media history of the refugee image, documents the role refugee artistic production plays in forming and negotiating geopolitical identities, and considers why aesthetics matter in a moment when the refugee is not tied to a singular event but instead is a constituent feature of the contemporary global landscape. I turn to the Southeast Asian American population not because they are the initial or necessarily the most important refugee population but because they entered their receiving country's imagination *only* as refugees.[5] Due to the intimate visual way viewers in the United States were receiving the Vietnam War and following its refugees, when the real Southeast Asian people arrived American viewers were predisposed to approach this population as if they were the refugee characters who had climbed right out of the television drama of the Vietnam War. As viewers had precious little knowledge about this population beyond the singular aesthetic viewpoint that presented these characters as tired, helpless, and needy, the refugee identity came to circumscribe the Southeast Asian migrants when they entered the country. An iconic and enduring case study, the Southeast Asian American example therefore demonstrates how totally the refugee image can affect the cultural, ethnic, and racial positioning of a population, while also offering a wide array of media examples that illuminate how the refugee aesthetic is deployed, battled over, and rewritten.

Of course, the Vietnam War was not just about Vietnam, as all of Southeast Asia was included in the disruption, destruction, and decolonial energy brought forth by the war. Hmong, Cham, Cambodian, and Lao lands and people were heavily involved in wartime operations, creating multiple refugee populations, while Thailand, Malaysia, Indonesia, and the Philippines were often the first places where refugees landed, in addition to being sites of U.S. military operations. Conceptualizing "Southeast Asia" as a distinct and related group of nations is itself a legacy of imperial intervention, as Fiona Ngô, Mimi Thi Nguyen, and Mariam Lam opine: "*Southeast Asia* names a geographic region first conceived of as a geopolitical concern by the post–Second World War development of the military-intellectual complex, and subsequently reimagined by various Cold War and post–Cold War strategies of foreign policy, including catastrophic campaigns of bombings and regime changes that promised to resonate for decades to come."[6] They add that Southeast Asia serves as "a marketizing economy, a tourist destination, a dream of homeland or sometimes nightmare, a neoliberal state, a war or series of images about war, and more,"[7] recognizing that Southeast Asia exists as a complex object of knowledge, war, and pleasure that far exceeds standard juridical and political borders.

The Refugee Aesthetic builds on this insight by taking Southeast Asian *America* as the physical, psychic, and political figuration created when the complex geographic structure of Southeast Asia is reimagined as a constituent element of various U.S. national spaces. Centering the experiences of Southeast Asian American refugees, who form and continue to redefine the iconic images of the refugee in the contemporary moment, attends to this imaginative energy, the legacies of colonialism, and the "ongoing renewal"[8] of U.S. empire. Following in Ngô, Nguyen, and Lam's footsteps, I see this perspective as a way to further world Asian American and Asian studies[9] while articulating how, instead of responding to received governmental borders, Southeast Asian American artists are actively reimagining Southeast Asian America as an important ground for their U.S. spatial orientation. Moving from the well-worn position of the solitary exile to the collective identity of refugees, Southeast Asian American authors rewrite nostalgic critical characteristics of exilic literature by focusing on the new land as the site of present and future social critique. I propose that this contemporary body of literature both invites and critiques dominant host cultures by historicizing and elongating the refugee condition so that the past provides the material perspective to critically engage with refugees' current position in the American imagination. This book, then, is a call to revisit situated populations with subjects who express their particular form of belonging through their aesthetic forms.

Examining the aesthetic legacy of the Southeast Asian American refugee experience requires reflecting on how it is deployed to bureaucratically and racially position present-day populations who are seeking entry into the United States and Europe. I concur with Cathy J. Schlund-Vials's argument that "situated adjacent a contemporary backdrop of war and militarized displacement, Southeast Asian American studies generally, and critical refugee studies specifically, emerge as *necessary* interdisciplines to more deeply contemplate the current Syrian refugee crisis vis-à-vis history, archive, and methodology."[10] In *The Refugee Aesthetic*, taking an interdisciplinary critical refugee studies approach[11] is important for scrutinizing how and when certain groups, populations, and figures move in and out of the refugee position. And indeed, this approach recognizes that the refugee aesthetic has conventionally been used to create refugee positions that signify otherness, positions that are set against and conceptually reinforce the rootedness of national subjects. As opposed to other transnational subjects such as exiles, economic migrants, and cosmopolitans, the refugee, as an idea, also endows the receiving nation with a sense of benevolence that forces the refugee into a position of endless debt and/or gratitude. However, denaturalizing the relationship between refugee aesthetics and the refugee position recognizes that refugee aesthetics are flexible, created and utilized by refugees, nonrefugees, and institutions alike, and thus hold the potential to create other utopian, or perhaps dystopian, arrangements in the present and future.

One of the fundamental premises underlying *The Refugee Aesthetic* is that refugees are not just powerless objects of study and legislation but can also be theorists, critics, and culture makers. Attending to how artists in the Southeast Asian American diaspora face the legacy of empire in the neoliberal present is needed, as a lack of attention to the particularities of their diasporic aesthetic production and sociopolitical experience has allowed for the proliferation of narratives claiming that refugees smoothly assimilate into new lands through education, discipline, and hard work.[12] These narrow representations ignore their economic and academic marginalization, often reinforcing myths of Western exceptionalism, which is disconcerting for the international community at large, as the rhetoric of American hospitality and benevolence is used to validate military, economic, and cultural interventions throughout the globe. Reading refugee narratives in a manner that does not privilege or substantiate American benevolence reveals the ways in which many Southeast Asian American artists scrutinize Western orders of aesthetic judgment while indexing the unfulfilled promises of the democratic capitalist state.

Consequently, this book shows that while the American appetite for palatable difference has compelled refugee authors to include agreeable cultural touchstones in their work, refugee literature in particular appeals to aesthetics in order to reset the terms of transnational cultural contact. As Asian American studies ages, it is imperative to recognize unacknowledged styles and modes, and examining the refugee aesthetic is an opportunity to consider the forms and strategies used in refugee writing that do not always announce themselves as such and thus are not read within a larger body of refugee work. This book, then, invites us to revisit the literatures of migration and diaspora more generally to figure out where, how, and by whom refuge is being claimed.

The Aesthetic Tradition

Considering the abundance of pressing material matters central to refugee life, why, then, turn to aesthetics? And what can a focus on aesthetics offer a study of Southeast Asian American refugee life in particular, as modern aesthetics have often been accused of being an important tool in the othering of different people, subjects, and forms of thought. Terry Eagleton, for example, has famously shown that the rise of modern aesthetics codified the middle-class man as the presumed "universal subject" through a series of taste practices and procedures that centered European male personhood,[13] and many postcolonial theorists have long been suspicious of aesthetics and aesthetic theory, as they "see aesthetics as implicated in the canonical marginalization of postcolonial literatures."[14] Yet despite the contentious development and deployment of aesthetics as an intellectual concept, it is difficult to argue that something like a "postcolonial aesthetic" does not exist, particularly as "the aesthetic" concerns the form, value, and reception of artistic works. Because postcolonial literature draws from a vast range of different countries, people, and subject positions, obviously there is no such thing as a singular postcolonial subject; however, the presentation, marketing, and critique of work that comes from postcolonial nations has created a readership that expects and values certain generic conventions and literary styles from authors who hail from postcolonial parts of the globe.

Similarly, the Southeast Asian American authors and artists examined in this book did not create the refugee aesthetic; rather, they engage a refugee aesthetic that already exists. Refugee authors differ from their postcolonial kin in that refugees are formed through a very specific legal category imbued with qualitative aesthetic parameters that encourage a pattern of storytelling that lingers well past the moment when refugees enter into a country. With the 1951 United Nations Convention Relating to the Status of Refugees stating that refugees have to demonstrate that they have a well-founded fear of persecution,[15] April Shemak argues that "those seeking asylum must become eloquent, persuasive speakers despite the enormous obstacles that can hinder testimony,"[16] as they are required to construct themselves as refugees through a narrative performance. Even though some refugees disassociate themselves from the refugee experience by attempting to assimilate into the general population as quickly as possible, refugees still must define and construct themselves along with, or in contrast to, this legal category that generates visual and verbal styles of storytelling and presentation. Insofar as aesthetics can be considered the deliberate shaping of content into form, this discursive imperative is an aesthetic force, and its navigation creates aesthetic methods. In this light, while refugee aesthetics are usually unacknowledged in favor of more urgent matters of refugee life, aesthetics circumscribe refugee experiences, shaping everyday and artistic interactions that follow the refugees into the new land, providing a presumed standard or basis for how one qualifies as a refugee, and oftentimes displaying the intergenerational forms, prejudices, and legacies of refugee life that bind one refugee generation to the next.

The recent embrace of writing from the refugee position is an acknowledgment that this particular position provides an opportunity to create artwork that exceeds an immediate humanizing of refugees or a factual retelling of refugee experience. Creating refugee artwork can provide both the distance and the elongation of time necessary to reveal the commonalities, relations, and sensibilities that are obscured by the immediacy of experience and utilitarian information. As Christopher Lee proposes through his reading of Theodor W. Adorno, art and artworks can offer "an alternative to 'established fact' due to [their] embattled [and embedded] relationship with society,"[17] providing an important counterpoint to what is perceived to be "the real." By appearing to stand apart from yet also being a product of everyday life, literary and artistic works provide an illusionary coherence of the world, whereby a different kind of knowledge—an aesthetic knowledge—distinct from empirical fact is produced. This valuable aesthetic knowledge still requires careful interrogation, however, as aesthetics and aesthetic judgments retain structures that mirror and oftentimes work to reinforce hierarchical orders of any given society. Understanding aesthetic structures as complex and volatile forms, *The Refugee Aesthetic* approaches refugee artwork by keeping in mind Kandice Chuh's definition of aesthetics as "the processes and the structures of value making by which certain sensibilities become common sense and others are disavowed, subjugated, and otherwise obscured."[18] Connecting refugee aesthetics and politics, this book draws its methodological inspiration from the work of Edward Said to argue that aesthetic critique requires detailing *how* a particular group is narrated into history and, in the same breath, identifying *who* has the power to do so.[19]

Upsetting regimes of common sense requires an appeal to what Mikhail Bakhtin calls "the emotional-volitional tension of form,"[20] whereby Southeast Asian American refugee artworks express something to the reader/viewer that extends beyond the materiality of the artwork itself and its content, creating excessive meanings and mythological structures across different reading/viewing communities. Specifically, I want to consider how these mythological structures create and shape representations of the refugee experience, as these representations are both products and prime fashioners of the relationship between commonsense sensibilities and those that are disavowed. The tension between formal expectations and the desire for more excessive and expressive forms of meaning is a central theme in Sau-Ling Wong's groundbreaking analyses of Asian American literature and a defining characteristic of what Min Hyoung Song describes as "seemingly conventional" contemporary works of Asian American literature where "one finds a subtle but unmistakable commentary on their own form, a restless relationship to its traditions and a ceaseless search for another order of connection to its possible alternative pasts leading to more open presents."[21] Drawing from the conclusions of Chuh, Wong, and Song, I suggest that Southeast Asian American authors writing from the refugee position attend to the aesthetics and politics involved in representing the refugee experience but do not replace it with another singular refugee aesthetic. Instead, they use conventional narratives, stereotypes, and histories as platforms for their own aesthetic excursions. Their work actively interferes with reading practices, values, and expectations while simultaneously embracing and rejecting multiculturalism's pedagogical promise by offering different sensibilities that are not usually expected from refugees. By highlighting and restaging these encounters, refugee literature can reposition, reimagine, and creatively use minor sensibilities to rewrite aesthetic structures and values that produce the relationship drawn between the dominant and minor positions.

Tracking how refugees are presented illuminates the tropes that define and confine the ways that refugees are conventionally imagined. Specifically, through charitable appeals and associated forms of media coverage, refugees are most commonly filmed, photographed, and written about as "those who suffer." And while this display has been important for agencies and charitable administrators in reaching potential donors, this aesthetic regime has come to shape what refugees are and have to continue to be in order to be accepted and read as refugees. This performance, which is thoroughly embodied and persists long past when the legal refugee designation is made, draws attention to refugees themselves, shifting attention away from the capriciousness through which refugee categories are defined, practiced, and enforced by the state and ignores the geopolitical considerations that determine why refugees from one country are accepted over those from another country. While those seeking asylum come from a wide variety of places and do so for a multiplicity of reasons, refugees become a coherent type of person as they experience and represent the rigorous refugee process. Despite the variety of motivations and circumstances involved in qualifying for refuge, they come to embody refugee subjecthood, both physically and psychically, through the aesthetic, institutional, and interpersonal patterns that coalesce and create the refugee position. As refugees forge narratives about themselves in receiving countries, commonalities across ethnicities are formed through a recognition of the many hardships and the "enduring consciousness of [their] debt,"[22] but by representing these experiences artistically, refugee narratives also produce unique forms of beauty, critical consciousness, and utopian thinking.

As such, while refugee aesthetics brings together (and at times conflates) differing experiences, it also creates the opportunity for two interrelated outcomes. First, it draws a continuous line between otherwise disparate examples of persecution and marginalization, bringing attention to the humanistic need to address underlying structures that place and displace humans in a global world. Second, refugee aesthetics draws attention to the ongoing condition of the refugee experience, where feeling like a refugee and inhabiting the refugee position continue long after the bureaucratic political designation expires. Expressing the ongoing condition of the refugee experience requires a poetic voice, as the contradictions and hardships of refugee life are increasingly held in the body and the psyche, particularly as they linger and transform over years and generations. Yet refugee literature is similar to postcolonial, ethnic American, and women's literature insofar as it is often read and valued for offering up a way of life rather than artistic innovation, suggesting that it should be "studied in terms of authenticity, racism, and resistance rather than literariness per se."[23] The contemporary refugee artists studied in this book are fully aware that the commercial value of their artistic output depends on the instrumental routing of their work by other agencies and people. Part of the current refugee aesthetic style is a reflective anticipation of these circuits of literary reception and a subsequent positioning of their work as tools of aesthetic engagement rather than objects served up for aesthetic judgment. Displaying different sensibilities can appeal to a reader's ethnographic eye and can help in justifying the inclusion of refugee work as a distinct artistic category, but by highlighting the *values* that particular aesthetics and sensibilities carry, refugee artists can set the tone of this engagement even if, like all artists, they are never entirely sure of the ultimate outcome of this arrangement.

As refugees, the demand to explain one's presence began when Southeast Asian bodies were carefully documented in a series of refugee camps and continued as these migrants settled in the United States, making this group of refugees well skilled in constructing aesthetic styles that explained both their presence and where they wanted to go. Because of the political valence of the Vietnam War and the suspicion that followed the physical reminder of this Western imperial failure, Southeast Asian American refugees continually had to explain why their bodies had entered these new spaces, leaving present-day Southeast Asian American artists well prepared to tell their unique refugee histories. Born into an aesthetic tradition where institutions produce more narratives of refugee life than refugees themselves do, these refugee artists are used to aesthetic regimes that often work around, if not against, their individual interests. Due to the repeated presentation of differing refugee groups as downtrodden, tired, and helpless, viewers are apt to read refugees themselves as interchangeable, and whether through the persistent mother-child dyad or as an overflowing mass of people, refugee artists must continually fight being presented as symbols of abstract humanity by inventing the platforms, themes, and narrative techniques required to present their individual concerns.

Conventionally, the audience's perspective is centered and their interests are appealed to, luring them into thinking that they are responsible for the evaluation of asylum seekers—that it is they who must pass judgment on these situations, images, and people—when instead the decisions about refugees are made by immigration agents and diplomatic state interests. This misplaced belief in their own power to decide is generated in part by the portrayal of the refugee as "a victim whose judgment and reason had been compromised by his or her experiences,"[24] who therefore has to be spoken for by professionals, such as doctors, academics, and outreach agents, who are seen as being outside the situation and therefore not infected by the horrific experiences that make refugee testimony seemingly unrepresentable and unreliable. When considering that refugees come from a seemingly out-of-control environment, viewers/readers can feel as if they must constantly be on guard for misinformation and that they bear some responsible in guiding the refugee narrative into a "rational" setting. As Liisa Malkki argues, because of the roles created by these viewing structures, when refugees present as calm and rational actors, they are often seen as less "worthy" of assistance—in short, they are read as not real refugees.

In response, Southeast Asian American refugee authors have remained unyielding and recalcitrant in documenting the contradictions faced in their everyday lives. Expressing these contradictions can be read not only as registering unheard complaints but also as a way to detail refugees' societal roles, possibilities, and responsibilities, demonstrating their extensive knowledge of the U.S. context that they inhabit. This iteration of refugee aesthetics is remarkably rooted, often telling tales of marginalization but with the force and urgency of someone who understands that they are here to stay. Phuong Tran Nguyen describes this statement of "staying" as the product of a "refugee nationalism," which in the U.S. setting "has represented not so much a refusal to assimilate but rather a particular mode of becoming American—becoming Refugee American."[25] Becoming "Refugee American" articulates a sense of patriotic pride toward the United States but does so by highlighting the act of *becoming*—the unfinished process of being a refugee and an American. That is, even though the legal definition of a refugee describes a provisional status, the refugee subjectivity stays active by producing narratives that continually detail the qualities, thoughts, and social values of refugees across differing classes, genders, and generations.

Phuong Tran Nguyen contends that "good refugees" are supposed to look to a future where they will become unmarked Americans, standing as emblems of U.S. benevolence and its "victory" over communism. However, there are also the "bad refugees" who are unable to "get over" the past and dwell on the politics of the former land and/or cannot move on from the refugee passage. The difference between these two categories is directly related to the usefulness that refugee stories and positions have for the receiving state, where "good refugees" will ultimately assimilate and be held up as successes, while the "bad" ones will "fail" because they are "stuck in the past." That refugee subjectivity is read through such a stark bifurcation of two rigid categories indicates that refugees have a lack of control over the stories being told about them, as Viet Thanh Nguyen relates: "If you are not in power in your society because you're marginalized in some way, the terms of your representation are not up to you. And, as always, the terms of your representation are always going to be polarized into 'good' and 'bad.' Because you always have to prove that you're 'good,' and being good means being exceptional."[26]

In this light, the everyday-life material offered by authors such as Angie Chau, Bich Minh Nguyen, and Lac Su are important incursions into refugee aesthetics, as they contribute to the narrative plenitude needed to nuance and pluralize the bifurcated refugee subjectivity while showing how both the good and bad of refugee life often expresses itself in mundane ways rather than having to always be exceptional. Locating refugee life on this micropolitical level identifies common ground and intergenerational ties that exist between differing refugee groups, which are not always concerned with or directly created by state interests.

Agency, Audience, and Authenticity

In her 1943 essay "We Refugees," Hannah Arendt relates that refugees have trouble finding receptive audiences for their stories because "nobody likes to listen to all that; hell is no longer a religious belief of a fantasy, but something as real as houses and stones and trees. Apparently nobody wants to know that contemporary history has created a new kind of human beings—the kind that are put in concentration camps by their foes and in internment camps by their friends."[27] Even when audiences are willing to listen, the refugees' stories are not read merely as personal autobiographical sketches and instead take on broad, often contentious, political meanings in new cultural climates. Positioned as tellers of unwelcome truths, refugees are conditioned to internalize their "real" stories and tell comfortable or comforting ones in their place, as extensively detailing their experiences and expressing the variety of feelings that they may have about refugee life can compromise their ability to discreetly live in new lands. The uncertainty surrounding their reception, then, compels refugees to heavily tailor their stories to the needs and desires of their audience, with contextual demands requiring that these accounts be marked by stylized patterns of authenticity.

Yet in a provocative response to this conservative structure of refugee storytelling, decorated Vietnamese American author Monique Truong offers that Bình, the unreliable narrator in her masterwork *The Book of Salt,* is "a fuck you" to a reader who is "coming to the work thinking that you're going to find authenticity and a vessel of racial pain. [Instead] you're going to encounter a narrator who is lying all the time, and it serves him to tell you what he wants to tell you."[28] This literary interjection resists the lure of trading off of marketable difference and instead attends to the complex narrative decisions that Bình (and, by proxy, Truong) are compelled to make by having him "lie" to the reader, foregrounding the right of refusal and highlighting discursive agency. She introduces, or rather selectively offers, the reader of Southeast Asian American refugee literature a character who does not authentically display himself so that his experiences can be consumed and added to the cultural cache of the reader but instead strategically releases information for *his* own benefit.

This act of taking control of a narrative is significant for Southeast Asian American refugee writers and actors who have a long history of their narratives being used by colonial institutions, refugee organizations, and/or collaborative autobiographies cowritten by white authors. Truong has argued that these "organizing texts depended and thrived upon the 'authority' and/or 'authenticity' of the Vietnamese American voices/texts to bolster their own textual arguments,"[29] while the "different truth-content" offered by these voices is positioned to be in service of institutional narratives, usurping the intentions of "the respondent's original speech/narrative act."[30] In this light, the Vietnamese American voices that audiences receive are heavily shrouded by the cowriters' decision-making process and/or the needs of outside institutions. Included for "what they say" and not "how they say it,"[31] these kinds of refugee stories impede the development of a Vietnamese American literary voice, and, more broadly, the creation of a coherent Vietnamese American aesthetic vision.

Overwhelmingly entering the United States as a population of refugees, the initial wave of Southeast Asian immigrants did not have certainty about which country they would go to and hence were provided only a limited amount of linguistic training in new languages,[32] resulting in a limited number of books written in English by Vietnamese American authors. The first generation, then, was left to construct oral narratives, and despite their initial dispersal to various parts of the United States, a distinct style was able to emerge. As Nhi T. Lieu notes, with this group there was a conscious decision made to fight the image of the refugee, the nameless hoard of boat people that filled the pages of *Time* and *Reader's Digest* in the late 1970s and early 1980s, as it was important for many Vietnamese migrants to assert their material and communal success to both Americans and Vietnamese populations.[33] The 1.5-generation authors, by contrast, have grown up in the United States and are equipped with the language skills and cultural capital to tell stories of refuge and refugee life in a manner that earlier generations could not. The burden and opportunity for this new generation of writers, though, is to construct new identities and communities in ways that deal seriously with the material and psychic effects of the traumatic passage and conditions of their immigration without reducing all Vietnamese American experience to this one event. Indeed, the first book-length study of Vietnamese American literature, Isabelle Thuy Pelaud's *This is All I Choose to Tell* (2010), highlights strategic acts of disclosure as an important practice and style for refugee speakers: some information is kept private and away from rote interpretive practices but in such a way that the refugee does not have to perform absolute silence. Translating the encounter between the interviewer and respondent into audience and artist, refugee experience is no longer something to be surrendered to an aggressive and coercive interlocutor, and the act of negotiating the release of information can be reconsidered as a political and aesthetic act that the refugee consistently performs.

Centralizing refuge, on their own terms, is an important tactic for authors who want to assert their difference, or at the very least their particularity, from the population they left behind, a fact that is often obscured when their work is being promoted or reviewed. Indeed, Pelaud notes that reviewers "often blur the distinction between being Vietnamese American and Vietnamese," ignoring details of cultural dislocation in favor of marketing authors' experiences as beguilingly exotic.[34] Southeast Asian

American writers also face an abundance of narratives produced about the Vietnam War that revolve around the concerns of American war veterans and state agencies, leaving little space for Southeast Asian American voices. Michele Janette contends that "Vietnamese American literature engages this erasure both in writing about Vietnamese perspectives on that war, and by expanding the signification of 'Vietnam' beyond being a synonym for a war."[35] Refuge, then, provides a place where Southeast Asian American authors can assert their different experiences and form a position where they are not just voices from Vietnam but are also rooted subjects who can critique different ideological systems and forms of representation that position them as perpetual foreign threats.[36] While these refugees were created by a war, refugee aesthetics offers Southeast Asian American writers the opportunity to edit, explain, and contest their place both within and beyond the wartime narrative.

As Viet Thanh Nguyen enjoys the privileges of being a lauded professor and Pulitzer Prize–winning writer, when he takes the position of the refugee it is a matter of choice. Recognizing that the convergence of legal, visual, and temporal signifiers work together to define "a refugee," his success makes it possible for him to put on and discard this status when he chooses:

> I was once a refugee, although no one would mistake me for a refugee now. Because of this, I insist on being called a refugee, since the temptation to pretend that I am not a refugee is strong. It would be so much easier to call myself an immigrant, to pass myself off as belonging to a category of migratory humanity that is less controversial, less demanding, and less threatening than the refugee.[37]

While the refugee is an immigrant, Nguyen identifies the emotional valence and complexity that the term "refugee" carries when compared to other migratory characters—much like Arendt recognized seventy-five years prior. The very appearance of refugees can disrupt the relationships, privileges, and comforting ideologies of rooted life, and therefore the refugee condition is expected to exist as an exceptional and temporary phenomenon: a blip, where both those in the receiving country and refugees themselves will agree to forget the past in order to allow refugees to exist "just" as immigrants. While the broader refugee community may at times be amenable to this deal, the refugee writer is tasked with remembering and reintroducing the refugee into the collective consciousness, again and again, so that the complex patterns, structures, and contradictions of refugee life remain present.

However, the 1.5-generation refugee writer who can tell stories without the problematic coauthoring mediation that Truong deplores oftentimes has little memory of the actual event of refuge and therefore must seek creative ways to present this experience. Having arrived in the United States at four years old himself, for Nguyen being a "refugee writer" requires representing events that he can barely remember at all, a task further complicated by the fact that he cannot access "the voices of all the refugees who shared the exodus with me and did not make it, or did not survive."[38] In this light, even relying on the stories told to him by those elders who actively experienced refuge is not sufficient to produce a complete or "authentic" story, as it omits the experiences of the many who died and were left behind. Nguyen approaches this quandary by appealing to minor aesthetic sensibilities and relational positions, musing "if I can imagine them, then maybe I can hear them. That is the writers' dream, that if only we can hear these people that no one else wants to hear, then perhaps we can make you hear them, too."[39] Making an audience hear voices they do not want to hear and making them hear these voices in a manner that may make the audience uncomfortable demands a deft aesthetic touch, a forcefulness, and indeed a will that is uncompromising about what and how refugee stories are told. This stylistic approach suggests that Nguyen's choice to be a refugee writer is a call to actively and imaginatively restage refugee life, leveraging his 1.5-generation Vietnamese American voice to reveal the power imbalances embedded in conventional images of refugees, publish stories without white coauthoring, and appeal to audiences without foregrounding authentic experiences.

While some refugee writers prefer to be "invisible" or see themselves as belonging to populations of "good refugees" who uniquely deserved refuge,[40] Nguyen and many other refugee authors are drawn to the position because they believe in their "human kinship to Syrian refugees and the 65.6 million people that the United Nations classifies as displaced people."[41] Few capture the deep sense of responsibility that comes from the refugee position as elegantly as Vu Tran:

> I had moved on from the circumstances that brought me to America and into the life it had given me and continues to give me. But America itself never quite moves on. The country of refuge never does, regularly stirred by new conflicts that remind it of the old ones. It keeps remembering your tragic origins, no matter how successfully you've embraced and achieved the promises it initially offered. On the street, it might no longer recognize the refugee in you, but the tide of American history continually washes new versions of you onto these shores, and their shadow is your shadow too.[42]

For Tran, feeling like a refugee is tough to shake because the structures that create and react to refugee people endure. Understanding that he shares a "shadow" with other refugees, Tran imparts that being a refugee has "informed how I see myself, how I see others see me, and how I want to be seen."[43] This recognition—and the receiving country's inability to move on—continually produces new refugee ties across national, racial, and ethnic lines, and the global political system ensures that the production of new refugees will continue. Embracing the refugee position, for Tran, provides the "personal fluidity" necessary to be outward-looking and inclusive when writing and pulling together the disparate elements of the refugee experience to create his own stories of refugee life.[44]

Refugee life in the contemporary moment is anything but a state of exception and as such has its own styles, patterns, and energy. To distinguish the role that refugee aesthetics plays during the twenty-first century, I have identified four key forces that shape how refugees are represented and received—the refugee image, the refugee position, refugee space, and the refugee personality—and have divided the book accordingly. In Chapter 1, "The Refugee Image," I examine the visual legacy of the Southeast Asian refugee experience, taking music videos, graphic novels, and refugee artwork as points of departure to investigate how cultural documents aestheticize detention, boats, bodies, waiting, and resettlement and how these depictions cumulatively mark which groups of people qualify as refugees in the global imagination. This chapter reviews the aesthetic connotations that fashion each designation, considers the potential outcomes and consequences of various approaches to visual representation, and theorizes how the refugee aesthetic is deployed to bureaucratically and racially position present-day refugee populations seeking entry into the United States and Europe.

Chapter 2, "The Refugee Position," turns more substantively to the cultural interventions that refugee artists make by examining how and why recent Southeast Asian American writers look to the refugee position to disentangle their complicated aesthetic legacy. Unlike refugees eager to leave the unsavory prejudicial connotations of the refugee image behind, these Southeast Asian American artists revisit the material pressures experienced by the first wave and reposition the critical dispositions found in exilic literature. This chapter proposes that new refugee aesthetic styles respond to the demand to explain one's presence, gesture toward social identities, and articulate a future for all refugee communities that acknowledges the lasting qualities engendered by the refugee experience.

Chapter 3, "Refugee Space," reorients the diasporic trajectory back out from the American continent to consider how refugees map and transform space. This chapter identifies new forms of refugee geography and recognizes how the imaginative force of places, such as the boat, oceans, and refugee camps, position Southeast Asian American lives in the global imagination. Through a close examination of Aimee Phan's novel *The Reeducation of Cherry Truong* (2012), I review Phan's unique projection of "Asian America" as a stylized Asian American suburban-style development built in Vietnam, to contemplate the existence of refugee space in everyday contexts. While Phan's imaginative construction proposes another future for refugee space and reminds us that new spaces are inevitable, it also describes a settler colonial impulse that discursively creates empty space at the expense of native inhabitants.

Chapter 4, "The Refugee Personality," explores Viet Thanh Nguyen's strategic deployment and refashioning of the refugee position into a subversive intellectual stance by analyzing the success of his Pulitzer Prize–winning book *The Sympathizer*. Paying close attention to Nguyen's own performance as a visible Vietnamese American author and academic, I track how he is positioned in reviews of his book while also noting how he negotiates his dual role during interviews and publicity tours. I argue that as a doggedly reflexive writer, Nguyen actively bleeds the material conditions of literary creation into the book itself by mapping patterns of taste, representational histories, and the perils of strategic exoticism, educating readers, editors, and interviewers through his creative craftwork.

The book concludes with "Refugee Futures," a reflection that considers what happens to refugee aesthetics now that it has also grown into a literary and artistic style that is identifiable and usable by nonrefugee artists. I explore in what ways this proliferation of refugee aesthetics both empowers and displaces refugee authors, and I query what this artistic attention will mean for refugees in the future, particularly since refugee populations will seemingly continue to increase in number and diversify in ethnic makeup.

The Refugee Aesthetic argues that the close examination of refugee aesthetics is necessary to track how the refugee category functions as fodder for political polemics. Refugee designation and admission is limited to particular groups, and therefore the refugee project "remains not so much a wholesale humanitarian endeavor"[45] as an exercise in state construction that selects incoming people on the basis of ideology, political affiliation, and race. Drawing from sociologist Randy Lippert, Yến Lê Espiritu contends that "during the Cold War years, '*refugeeness* became a moral-political tactic,' demarcating the difference between the supposed uncivilized East and the civilized West and fostering a 'cohesion of Western Alliance nations'" where the "paradigmatic refugee was the East European and Soviet escapee."[46] The Southeast Asian American refugee population thus signaled a dramatic turn in the image of who refugees were, recoding this category with racial connotations that mixed together war, communism, and Asianness. In this light, the aestheticized pattern of contemporary refugee reformation should be read as a racial drama in addition to a political one. As Mimi Thi Nguyen notes, the refugee narrative is one of "progress" that "target[s] the subject of freedom—the new friend who becomes the new arrival— through the concatenation of evolutionary and given times, developmental stages and universal humanity, and a temporalizing strategy,"[47] allowing for warmongering countries to point to "positive" outcomes and assert their benevolence through these endeavors. This powerful narrative posits that the refugee is brought forth from a dystopian past (which was in part fashioned by wars and systems of empire) before they are brought into "Western modernity." This dominant narrative framework positions the refugee as a renewable resource and a remarkably durable technology, telling a tale that provides a teleology of racial progress, reframes wars of aggression as humanitarian endeavors, and delivers the rhetorical infrastructure necessary for empire to pursue further wars.

This book, then, is about the politics of the refugee aesthetic, understanding that refugee expression has been cloaked in and produced by grand geopolitical narratives that focus on the refugee's reformation, a perspective that provides an alibi and a distraction for the continuation of imperial endeavors. Liberating refugee narratives and aesthetics from these confines does not produce social critique in and of itself but instead allows scholarly inquiry to examine refugee production on its own terms whether it challenges, avoids, or even reinforces these common geopolitical narratives. Recognizing the ways that refugee experiences are aestheticized should change the ways that refugees are conventionally thought of and can demonstrate how a greater flexibility of address, multiple subject positions, and an emphasis on interiority are currently shifting the focus from a singular refugee aesthetic to the complexity offered by refugee aesthetics. Refugee aesthetics is not a problem to be solved, in other words, but instead is a generative force that elongates the temporal coordinates of refugee life to reimagine the past, present, and future of this population in the world.

1

The Refugee Image

Recently, I had the pleasure of attending the opening of an art exhibit about the refugee experience that featured collaborative work created by a Syrian American artist and an Iraqi American writer, the latter of whom was a refugee himself. As they were new and not part of the usual academic or artistic circles that contemplate the refugee experience, I was interested in who they considered to be their aesthetic interlocutors and predecessors. So, during the question and answer period I asked if they drew upon other refugee artists when making their work. They responded, "No we did not. We did not really have anyone; there was no framework to draw upon." At first I was taken aback by their declaration, particularly considering how rich their own exhibit was in making connections across different refugee communities. However, the moment crystalized for me how the conventional rhetoric surrounding the refugee experience coerces one to see each refugee crisis as an isolated phenomenon without a comparable history or aesthetic. Each refugee group is apt to see its own experiences as particularly dire and exceptional, deserving of a distinct aesthetic presentation, while "forgetting" or at the very least diminishing the similarities found between their plight and the lives of refugees who came before them. This perspective is amplified by increasingly rapid media cycles, where in order to gain visibility in the global marketplace of images, one's own circumstances must be presented as uniquely disconcerting to draw attention and resources to the crisis at hand.

In an attempt to disrupt this precarious and pernicious line of thinking, this chapter demonstrates that while refugees themselves are, of course, quite diverse, the refugee *image* has been remarkably consistent in regard to its form. While the individuals inhabiting the refugee image may change, the form itself offers a collection of characteristics that have remained mostly stable since the Southeast Asian refugee crisis. And indeed, refugees themselves can bristle the flow of images produced over the past forty years that renders refugees interchangeable. This figuration of the refugee dehistoricizes particular refugee groups and is "inevitably a project of depoliticization," where the refugee image is prized for its use-value instead of its artistic worth or ability to describe the complexity of individuals who become refugees. This portrays a number of different experiences as uniform under the category of "refugee life" and creates a tension between refugees and the visual approaches that are meant to represent them.[1] In identifying the ways that refugees are conventionally represented in various media forms, this chapter considers the different possibilities involved in viewing those presented as refugees in order to determine both the uses and limitations of the refugee image while distinguishing its visual grammar.

The United Nations has determined that in order to qualify for refugee status, asylum-seeking migrants must demonstrate that they have a "well-founded fear of persecution," and April Shemak, in her book *Asylum Speakers* (2010), argues that this bureaucratic designation is achieved at least in part through a performance where asylum seekers must convince the gatekeepers that they in fact do have a well-founded fear of persecution. As all performances are created within communicative systems, the asylum seeker's discursive plea draws upon the performances generated by previous actors who sought asylum and requires potential refugees to anticipate the words, gestures, and behavioral styles that their audience expects.

These images and signs cumulatively form what a "refugee" is in the global imagination, which then, at a more local level, influences the human actors—border guards, government officials, lawyers, and so forth—who get to decide who qualifies for refugee status. As W.J.T. Mitchell argues, "Images 'go before' the immigrant, in the sense that before the immigrant arrives, his or her image comes first in the form of stereotypes, search templates, tables of classification, and patterns of recognition,"[2] which means that "the immigrant arrives as an 'image-text' whose documents go before him or her at the moment of crossing the border."[3] While Mitchell is concerned with documents such as passports and visas that must exist before immigrants can traverse a border, in this chapter I explore how refugees are marked by media aesthetics that turn their bodies into overdetermined forms of image-texts. Analyzing refugees as image-texts requires understanding what the characteristics of the refugee image are, what patterns of seeing are created by the refugee image, and how refugees negotiate the existing visual archive of the refugee experience when they start creating visual images of their own.

Moving Pictures: Image and Flow

Cumulatively, aesthetic patterns create the connotations that fashion the refugee designation, and differing immigrant populations are marked as economic migrants or political refugees in part through their visual legibility. While there had been refugee populations previously, the Southeast Asian refugee population, most specifically the so-called Vietnamese boat people, have emerged as *the* contemporary visual icons of the refugee experience, as they were subject to a particularly intimate and substantive layering of televisual and photographic images. Through the interplay of these two technologies, a visual regime developed that continues to shape the ways that subsequent refugee populations are read both in the United States and around the globe.

Consider how the music video for the song "Borders," written, directed, and performed by Tamil British rapper M.I.A., a refugee herself from the Sri Lankan Civil War (1983–2009),

Figure 1.1 M.I.A. music video for "Borders" (2015). © 2015 Maya Arulpragasam.

cleverly assembles and resituates a number of iconic representations of refugees that emerged during the Southeast Asian refugee era.[4] Her 2015 video reimagines key refugee image types that derive from the Southeast Asian example, highlighting the ways that boats, bodies, and masses inform contemporary considerations of refugees and the refugee position.

Harkening back to the so-called boat people crisis, the image in Figure 1.1 presents a literal conflation of boats and people, where a mass of cloaked men are arranged across the shoreline taking the shape of a freighter. Arranging their bodies in this orderly manner requires some to contort their bodies, while M.I.A. herself stands tall, impressively looking forward over the bow. In the video itself, the formation is presented with a panoramic sweep over the beach set against the breaking waves of the ocean, creating an unexpectedly majestic presentation of these newly styled "boat people," where the movements of water, bodies, and boat together comprise a powerful force.

The orderliness, movement, and majesty offered by Figure 1.1 contrast with the messy assemblage of bodies seen in a more customary take on refugee life found later in the video (Figure 1.2). Whereas in Figure 1.1 the people became a boat, in Figure 1.2 the boat itself takes the form of people. The cramped

Figure 1.2 M.I.A. music video for "Borders" (2015).
© 2015 Maya Arulpragasam.

arrangement of limbs, feet, and faces, splayed across every space of the deck, and the various askew gazes of the refugees who look off to the side evoke the refugees' mixture of boredom, suffering, and waiting. This overflowing tangle of weakened, placid bodies became a common motif in photojournalist accounts of the Vietnamese boat people, as in order to make the most money possible, Vietnamese intermediaries packed boats with an excessive amount of people, overwhelming the limits of the vessels. With most photographs of these boats taken from afar, the structure of the boats themselves was transformed visually into a hybrid of wood and degraded bodies, serving to mark the inhuman (or in some ways overly human) conditions that these refugees had to endure. When photojournalists were able to get closer to the subjects at hand, the presentation of the bodies and faces stylistically mirrored the image in Figure 1.2, where cramped bodies, with faces filled with suffering, helplessness, and endurance, look off in the distance.

Adrift, these faces and bodies portray the refugee experience as one of indeterminate waiting—for something, or someone, to change their station in life. But the refugee image, when presenting an overwhelming number of bodies, focuses attention on masses and multitudes rather than individuals.[5] In Figure 1.2 "the mass" is conveyed through overlapping bodies literally spilling off of the boat. This idea of a "flood of people" can also be translated into the photographic form by having the shot positioned so that refugees spill off of the sides of the frame. Liisa Malkki describes these photos as "spectacle[s] of 'raw,' 'bare' humanity" where oftentimes the bodies are so tightly packed that it occludes "that each of the persons in the photograph ... has a reason for being where he is now: inside the frame of the photograph."[6] Instead, the anxiety experienced by the refugees is partly transferred to the viewer who, overwhelmed by a series of unidentifiable faces, is tasked with surveilling each edge of the frame (and beyond) to find distinguishable markers among this flood of interchangeable people who await transformation into individuals.

Despite being commonly portrayed in a state of waiting, refugees are also depicted as an encroaching force through a technique that Leo Chavez identifies as the "directionality of movement."[7] Commonly, refugees are framed so that they are moving toward the camera, creating an effect where migrants are coming at the viewer and, by analogy, into their homes or lands. The rhetorical effect of this type of shot suggests potential danger and places both the viewer and the receiving nation as the place of *desire and decision making*.

The "directionality of movement" can be found in an iconic image (Figure 1.3), where a foregrounded family is coming ashore surrounded by a mass of boat people. While the strained facial expressions and the prominence of children paint a sympathetic portrait, framing this family amid a mass of indistinguishable people persuades the viewer that not only is the sympathetic family coming, but also a boat—of indeterminate size and length—filled with people who will soon seek shelter in the new land. Subtly countering sympathetic impulses, this photo positions the family, symbolically, as inhabitants of a Trojan horse who will open the door for others once they are able to find their way inside. Similarly, the "snaking line" provides directionality of movement but extends past the edge of the frame, creating what Chavez calls the "infinityline" that is "used to give the subtle but distinct impression that the flow of immigrants does not have a definitive end in sight, it simply goes

Figure 1.3 *Vietnam War.* Credit Jack Cahill/Toronto Star via Getty Images.

on to infinity."[8] Of course, as refugee populations, by definition, are characterized by distinct crises and legally refugee groups have a temporal beginning and end, this visual impression has little basis in reality. But the rhetorical effect of these techniques positions the viewer, the consumer, and the receiving country in a manner whereby they could conceive that they will *always* be the arbitrators of refugee populations, as this flood of people is seemingly endless.

As the refugee image provides an intense focus on a number of unfamiliar and often racially distant bodies, one of the lessons provided by the Southeast Asian refugee example is that with repetition, bodies themselves come to be seen as what requires transformation. Conventional representations of refugees focus on their lives, bodies, and rehabilitation, taking attention away from the geopolitical conditions that created them. Attending to the particulars of the refugee passage overlaps information and aesthetics in a manner such that the viewer can be attracted and sympathetic to refugees in the abstract but, at the same time, repulsed by the squalid living arrangements and uncomfortable politics that seem to follow refugees as they move from land to land. This contradiction positions the viewer as the decision maker, creating an illusion of responsibility where refugees are looking *at them,* coming toward them, waiting for a change, a decision, or judgment. The viewer is urged to mull over and consider the evidence presented before them and decide what they think should happen to the people in these images rather than considering their own position and complicity in the creation of refugee lives.

Instead of existing as a passive body of material that waits for the viewer to care, M.I.A.'s video repositions images of refugees as a ground for refugee recognition, consciousness, and empowerment. Her message is for refugees themselves to rise up as a force, and her aesthetic intervention is (seemingly) to position refugees as powerful consumers and creators of refugee images rather than conceding complete control over the images' production and dissemination to the settled citizens of receiving countries.[9] While alone M.I.A.'s provocation may not provide the lofty impact of an empowered refugee consciousness, this approach delivers a jarring contrast to the deluge of images of Syrian refugees circulating around the time of her video's release. By presenting images of suffering bodies and destitution, contemporary photojournalists and media cohorts sought to create a similar sense of visibility and sympathy for these Syrian refugees that the Southeast Asian refugees ultimately gained. For the images of the Vietnamese boat people were considered key documents that helped create the social pressure necessary for the United States to accept more Southeast Asian refugees in the late 1970s and early 1980s. But M.I.A.'s video suggests that this kind of appeal may be outmoded in the twenty-first century and that a rethinking of what refugees can signify is in order.

As David Campbell suggests, "the dream of photojournalism is that when a crisis is pictured the image will have an effect on the audience that will lead to action."[10] Indeed, this is the power of what philosopher and critic Jacques Rancière has called the "intolerable image,"[11] where violent images are transformed into a "recognition of humanity"[12] that "'restores the powers of attention itself.'"[13] Images of refugees at times can evoke this action, but often this straight line between crisis, image, and action goes off the rails. As the spectacle of the refugee image ages, one wonders about the power to create these intended responses if typical representative forms are repeated ad nauseam. When taken in sum—the boats and bodies, the waiting, the masses of people, and the directionality of movement—the underlying message of the refugee image is that refugee crises will be endless. The sheer number of similar images of degraded refugee life generated over time creates the impression that the refugees, these images, and the crises that produce refugees will never cease to end. This is tragic for the refugees, of course, but empowering in a way for the viewer, who is lulled into thinking that the qualities of refugee life are so diametrically opposed to what they experience that becoming a refugee will never happen to them. This distant viewer becomes complicit in a dubious kind of comfort where, with a seemingly infinite number of refugees being produced, they are provided with a limitless replay of a human drama they will endlessly get to watch.

To Look at Refugees: Uses and Meanings

As refugees themselves are a diverse group of people, the refugee image is not singular in terms of its content, yet images of refugees follow identifiable formal patterns because there are distinct and profitable *uses* of the refugee image. In other words, despite claims that these images organically bring to light a "common humanity" across different cultures, it is more accurate to say that this body of work has acquired consistency because of its ideological nature and the thematic coherence in interpreting, recording, and defining the events of refuge. So, while patterns of the refugee image are explained above, in this section I explore the ways that the refugee image circulates and is used to produce meaning. I pursue the word "image," as opposed to "picture" or "photograph," because it encompasses a variety of media products while allowing for both the study of representational apparatuses and the ways that images are received.

When an object is represented and lifted into an image economy it signifies across different times and contexts, allowing an object to live on in a multitude of ways. The refugee image has currency, as it allows individual refugee groups to be visualized in faraway places, and their plight is preserved in ways that allow for comparison across differing moments. A more postmodern approach would quibble with this mimetic language, nudging the critic to consider the play of images and image regimes over time, understanding that despite their promise to the viewer of an efficient and immediate view of somewhere, someone, or something else, images actively create meaning without the necessary recourse to referents. In this sense, an image is not a diminished or altered version of the thing itself but rather an object that lives on in its own right, circulating and creating its own distinct form and relations to other images.

To understand the image's own force one must attend to the circulation and flow of refugee images and recognize that viewing experiences are inexorably tied to the ways refuge is transmitted and communicated. With television, for instance, images appear in the home every day, cumulatively constituting a flow of events, experiences, and people. This is why television is often seen as building intimacy between the viewer and the viewed subject because it invites a group of strangers into one's own home. While intimacy can imply comfort and hospitality, Susan Sontag offers that the American war in Vietnam was "the first to be witnessed day after day by television cameras, introduc[ing] the home front to a new tele-intimacy with death and destruction."[14] As Southeast Asian refugees were the first refugees to be introduced in a televisual manner, there was an opportunity for a particularly amicable connection to be forged between viewers and this group of refugees. However, Sontag's insight reminds us that instead of arriving as a discrete set of images sympathetically portraying the hardships of individuals in flight, the refugee image was presented alongside images of violence. That is, Southeast Asian refugees entered homes through a flow of images that positioned them as the continuation of the death, destruction, and heartbreak of the Vietnam War. Accordingly, the Southeast Asian refugees were introduced as the dramatic denouement of a jarring, discomforting, and uncomfortable television narrative with an unsettling and uncertain plot.

When turned into images, refugee people are transformed into symbols of war, nationhood, and global culture, standing in as the trace of less visible political-economic structures such as capital, climate change, and empire. Because the refugee designation is a global matter, images of refugees are inextricably read as symptoms of large social structures, stirring the viewer to consider and interpret the presence of grand political and ethical forces when looking. Refugee images rouse more than just sympathy but carry a substantial amount of gravity, solemnity, and opportunity. These images traverse and help to redefine spaces that are strategically hidden by the state, drawing attention, aid, and/or persecution to people in detention sites while provoking questions about the nature and practice of state sovereignty and security. As migrants and refugees are increasingly held in offsite locations like the Naura Regional Processing Center and domestic detention centers are positioned out of public view, the image is vital in putting refugees on the map, forcing them into the global imagination even if they are considered to be marginal or "over there."

But what do refugee images do on the map? And what kind of attention do they draw? One possibility is that images of refugee degradation can shock an audience into action, with John Berger offering that images of atrocity remind the viewer of the lived experiences behind abstractions such as political theory and statistics, serving "as an eye we cannot shut."[15] This "eye that we cannot shut," however, is not an all-knowing perspective that brings the viewer into the world of suffering; on the contrary, "the moment of the other's suffering engulfs us," and when "we try to emerge from the moment of the photograph back into our lives . . . the contrast is such that the resumption of our lives appears to be a hopelessly inadequate response to what we have just seen."[16] Extrapolating from Berger's formulation, we can consider the possibility that the representation of refugee suffering and atrocity can create and/or extend the emotional and experiential gap between the viewer and the refugee by placing these refugees' lived experiences in a different world or "out of time."[17] While images may be meant to "awaken concern,"[18] the photograph creates a stark contrast between "the photographed moment and all others," where the "arresting" moment is not only the horror that is witnessed itself but also the viewer's feeling of paralysis when faced with a photograph that seems out of time or place. Berger concludes that the issues surrounding war and violence become depoliticized in such a moment, as the viewer does not pursue questions of governmental and institutional complicity and instead "his sense of shock is dispersed,"[19] turning attention away from global matters and back toward his/her own emotional well-being.

And it is not difficult to see how the shock of the refugee image can be dispersed on a large social scale as well. While the arresting image surrounding the death of three-year-old Alan Kurdi, the refugee boy from Syria who washed up on the shores of a beach in Turkey, produced a surge in donations to international refugee organizations, his death was quickly abstracted into a "human catastrophe" by then French president François Hollande,[20] a rhetorical move that accuses everybody and nobody at the same time. When used in this grandiose manner, the refugee image can again lengthen the perceived distance between the viewer and the image, mapping the spatial and temporal particulars of the tragedy so abstractly that these events seem even more extraordinary and remote from the viewer's own life than they would usually be. In this light we can understand Sontag's suggestion that horrific and difficult images produce a "double message" by showing "suffering that is outrageous, unjust, and should be repaired" yet at the same time "confirm[ing] that this is the sort of thing which happens in *that* place . . . [,] nourish[ing] belief in the inevitability of tragedy in the benighted or backward—that is, poor—parts of the world."[21] This distancing effect is so strong that when refugees enter a new country, a viewer inhabiting this receiving place could still read the refugee plight as something remote, as the image presents these bodies as symbols of a radically different space and therefore involved in a radically different state of being. In other words, even when the refugees themselves are not physically remote, the historical force of the refugee image can keep them seemingly distant and foreign.

Of course, refugee images are not only images of atrocity; they remain disorienting and uncomfortable because the viewer cannot find a place to enter the encounter. Unlike wartime photos, refugee images are not held up as a military achievement, as they do not exhibit the qualities of what Nerissa Marie Balce describes as the "monstrosity and magnificence of empire."[22] The refugee image does not provide the viewer with clear distinctions between "good" and "bad" and the ability to experience the clear joys of conquest or the devastation of defeat. Wendy Kozol and Susie Linfield suggest, respectively, that there is a productive ambiguity and ambivalence to the refugee image that requires the viewer to mull over the circumstances of refuge. Linfield offers that the image's density resists easy and quick conclusions, and instead "we might see [the image] as part of a process— the beginning of a dialogue, the start of an investigation—into which we thoughtfully, consciously enter."[23] But in invoking "the beginning of a dialogue," we must ask who is this dialogue with? Certainly not with the refugees, for they are cordoned off behind the image. It seems instead that the refugee image enables viewers to start an internal dialogue with themselves, provoking and probing their own place in the world, but it is less clear when and how the refugees will join this conversation. Further, understanding the *content* of the refugee image requires little dialogue or interpretation, as through its repetition it very clearly and simply alludes to a way of life. When Tom Petty growled in 1979 at the height of the Southeast Asian refugee crisis that "you don't have to live like a refugee,"[24] he was not using the image of a refugee to provoke contemplation about policy decisions or armed conflict but instead was merely deploying this figure to signify a state of being downtrodden. Even refugees themselves often want to flee the designation as quickly as possible to alleviate the social stigma that comes with the position, and therefore the overwhelming message of the refugee image for everyone involved—critics, viewers, and refugees alike—is that the refugee position should be a temporary one.

For instance, Edward Said and Jean Mohr's *After the Last Sky: Palestinian Lives* is an impressive attempt to speak for and present a population that is usually seen only through distant media coverage. Through a series of intimate portraits by Mohr with captions by Said, they replace the simple and harmful mass media representations of Palestinians with a capricious mix of the autobiographical, academic, and expressive voice.

Yet even when creating this complex picture of Palestinian life, they struggle find a place at the table for the Palestinian refugee image. Said's discomfort with the refugee image is palpable when he explains that "the image of a helpless miserable-looking refugee has been replaced by this menacing one [of the terrorist] as the veritable icon of 'Palestinian.'"[25] Skipping past the refugee image is an understandable gesture, as over time this motif of disempowerment and desperation has hardened into a stereotype that Said and Mohr are attempting to subvert. Yet in Said's eagerness to refute the new threat of the terrorist image, the refugee image again gets short shrift, is cast aside, and remains undertheorized by this master theorist. Reasonably, Said would rather concentrate his efforts on material global initiatives that would end refugee existence and refugee suffering rather than acknowledging them as a permanent entity.

When contemplating how the refugee image circulates and what it means, it becomes clear that while refugee images are seen to document extraordinary circumstances, they are also quite effective in normalizing a way of life. That is, despite the supposed urgency suggested by the content of the refugee image and the overwhelming international desire for refugees to be temporary, the image contains an internal contradiction where, over time, viewers can become accustomed to the ambivalence that these images create. In this light, refugees are no longer the result of a state of exception occurring on the world stage but instead, in the words of Trinh Thi Minh Ha, are "sadly an accepted part of everyday life."[26] Indeed, the idea of refugees has become so normalized that a team now competes under the refugee designation in the Olympics—an acknowledgment, or resignation, that refugee life is merely another competitor on the world stage. The dream of the refugee image is to make it intolerable for anyone to continue with their lives until the refugee crisis is solved. Yet the endurance of refugees, the stability of images, and a seemingly unending supply of crises make refugees a familiar and permanent guest as their pictures stream into people's homes. But where does this normalization leave those who are creating images from a refugee position? How can refugee artists and institutions take up artistic projects that work through this well-established circuit of reception? What options do they have to represent a life that is supposedly temporary but structurally endures?

Reframing Refugees

A consequence of being very visible as icons yet little known as American people is that Vietnamese American artists can use the familiarity of the Vietnamese refugee and the Vietnam War to reorient the consumption of refugee images. Instead of directly refuting the validity of the more iconic images, artists/authors can use them as entry points to provide intricate ruminations regarding the war's aftermath, diasporic Vietnamese life, and the unevenness of political representation. For instance, a section of Thi Bui's graphic narrative *The Best We Could Do* (2017) explores Eddie Adams's Pulitzer Prize–winning photograph *Saigon Execution* by considering the photo's orthodox usage, the myriad contexts involved in the execution, and the image's enduring effects on refuge life. Capturing the force of a South Vietnamese general, Nguyen Ngoc Loan, brutally shooting a Viet Cong prisoner through the head, *Saigon Execution* is conventionally understood as a photo that galvanized American opposition to the Vietnamese War, where even U.S. allies were seen as participating in barbaric acts. However, Bui disturbs this uncomplicated reading by presenting the photo as an object that stirred a recollection her refugee father has about his own trying encounters with Vietnamese police and military. In the text, Bui's autobiographical character figures out that the same general involved in her father's near arrest in Vietnam was responsible for the famous shooting. Yet when learning about this information, instead of using it as an opportunity to berate the general, her father criticizes the circulation of the famous photo, explaining that the shooting was in response to the Viet Cong prisoner murdering an entire family hours before the picture was taken.

Redrawing the famous photo herself, alongside her father's story, re-places this iconic image within the flow of her book and the multiple threads of family history that it contains, providing a differing circuit of meaning that is informed by but contrasts with the image's worldly media saturation. Like the rest of the book, the image is drawn in a single blood-colored wash that, Jocelyn Sakal Froese argues, explores "stories of immigration that involve blood, both literally (the Vietnam war, the blood present at birth) and figuratively (family lines, ethnicities, ethnic cleansing, racism)."[27] In Bui's book, *Saigon Execution* is one of many instances colored and covered by this blood-like imagery; however, the number of panels devoted to the picture's interpretation positions it as a dense nexus of meaning that sheds light on her family's history and refugee life more broadly, illuminating uses for the image that extend beyond a straightforward reflection about the U.S. war with Vietnam. The contrast between her father's memories and the typical American understanding of the shooting leads Bui to investigate what happened to the general after the political urgency of the image faded away. In seven panels, Bui's character explains that Eddie Adams later tracked down Nguyen Ngoc Loan, who was working a menial job in a pizza parlor in the United States, illustrating in Bui's words the general's "fall from grace." Through this exploration we glimpse how, without context, the *Saigon Execution* image falls from grace alongside the general as it is emptied of much of its relevance for most audiences; however, this image endures as a complicated and significant object for refugees such as Bui and her father.

Revisiting both the image and the general provides Bui with an opportunity to bring these degraded images and people back to life by having them flow through her family's history. Dogged acts of recontextualization and careful exposition allow her to oppose the limited and utilitarian manner in which refugee images are used. In particular, through a direct address to the reader, she comments on the uneven reading practices and contexts that surround images of Southeast Asians in the closing of the *Saigon Execution* section:

> 'Saigon Execution' is credited with turning popular opinion in America against the war. I think a lot of Americans forget that for the Vietnamese . . . the war continued whether America was involved or not. For my parents there was

a rocket that barely missed their house ... and killed a neighbor ... best friends and students killed in combat ... frequent periods of separation ... the constant stress of money ... the baby that dies in the womb ... and then my arrival ... three months before South Viet Nam lost the war.[28]

Attending to Vietnamese lives in this manner centers Vietnamese experiences that occurred during and after the war while bringing continuity to war, refuge, and resettlement. On a sociopolitical level, this refugee document brings colonialism, communism, U.S. intervention, and refuge together as a series of causal events, whereas they are otherwise represented as a set of discrete historic entities.

However, the act of weaving these threads together is not a given, requiring work and rigorous interpretation. And Bui takes the time to show her narrator piecing through her father's recollections while struggling to comprehend if her father hated the general and/or communist Vietnam. With two panels dedicated to her icon mulling over the stories with eyebrows furrowed, lost in thought, Bui juxtaposes the struggle involved in interpreting her own history alongside many mainstream images that circulate about the Vietnam War. She comments that "the contradictions in my father's stories troubled me for a long time. But so did the oversimplifications and stereotypes in American version of the Vietnam War." This latter sentence stands as a heading over the top of a panel where half of the frame consists of American soldiers alongside a caption reading "GOOD GUYS." Then there is a parallel panel of a barely visible soldier hiding in some brush titled "BAD GUYS—the Viet Cong (Communist Front in the South). Very hard to see" before concluding with a final panel that catalogs numerous stereotypes of South Vietnamese people, described as "bar girls and hookers," "papa-san," "kids looking for handouts," "small effete men," and "corrupt leaders."[29] This list of stereotypical characters and scenarios who played out the media drama of the Vietnamese War seem perversely broad when compared to the nuances of her father's story and out of place in this alternate

Figure 1.4 *The Best We Could Do* by Thi Bui.
© Abrams ComicArts.

realm of knowledge that Bui is presenting and developing. In foregrounding her own struggle in trying to put this story together, she suggests that the refugee experience itself involves the difficult work of putting these pieces together and models a form of knowledge production that revisits refugee images to produce more valuable ways of knowing and seeing than what is consumed through a mass media circuit.

GB Tran's graphic narrative *Vietnamerica: A Family's Journey* (2010) similarly focalizes on the task of reordering the past and interpreting a disrupted family history.[30] With the book's cover composed of a jigsaw of various faces, Tran attempts to create a transnational Vietnamese refugee history by reorienting the visual imagery of Vietnamese bodies, no longer presented as undifferentiated masses, and is able to harness the power of the graphic narrative to present a refugee story characterized by multivalence and relationality. In the graphic narrative Vietnamese bodies, gestures, and practices are produced in a dialectical relationship with their space, and as such *Vietnamerica* provides a staggering range of what Vietnamese people are and can be by routing them through multiple environmental contexts, while Vietnamese and Vietnamese American bodies are shown as agential figures that can sculpt their own spaces.

Traditionally, the comic book form has trafficked in crude stereotypes to quickly reach a paying audience, yet the quick connection between reader and text also presents the possibility to rapidly recode unsavory representations by reframing the body to produce a different and more particularized iconography.[31] With a wide array of visual options available to Tran, the narrative weight of the graphic text does not always need to be carried by the actors and figures themselves, and therefore visual displays of the bodies can be strategically deployed to capture the intricacies of their social presence. For instance, Tran uses the technique of spilling over, commonly used to present refugee masses, to a haunting effect in his graphic narrative *Vietnamerica* in Figure 1.5.

Figure 1.5 portrays bodies straining to get out of the cavernous outline of Vietnam during the period of refuge, where

Figure 1.5 Illustrations from *Vietnamerica: a Family's Journey* by GB Tran. Copyright © 2011 by Gia-Bao Tran. Used by permission of Villard Books, an imprint of Random House, a division of Penguin Random House LLC. All rights reserved.

through the technique of graphic bleeding the landscape spills over the page, illuminating the uncertainty that these bodies faced—fleeing the difficult past and dangerous present, desperately straining toward an uncertain future. The tiny boats that could transport them away are overwhelmed by the size of this social body, alluding to the images in Figures 1.1–1.4 of the Vietnamese refuge where an unthinkable number of people are crammed into these tight spaces and figures teem across the decks of the boats. The graphic weight of the image in Figure 1.5 focuses the gaze on Southeast Asia, while a dark fiery horizon characterizes the foreboding, unknowable, global north. The gloomy dull grays of Laos, Thailand, and Cambodia suggest that little hope is to be found in other lands, and hence the majority of the bodies cram themselves into the bottom of the frame desperately reaching into the crisp light blues of the ocean—a liquid respite that would carry them off the page into the unknown. However, while the faces are drawn rather crudely, Tran reinvests these people with a sense of individuality, as the lines of distress and horror are clearly visible, a diversity of hairstyles is apparent, and small identifiable ornaments such as glasses produce particularity before the bodies blend into a mass of humanity as the reader's eye travels northward.

The bodies in Tran's *Vietnamerica* retain their multiplicity, distinction, and liveliness through his use of synesthesia and subjective expressionistic techniques. His aesthetic intervention follows the visual lead of other Asian American graphic novelists such as Gene Luen Yang in using exaggerated physical movements to guide the reader. While conversations in the book tend to be simple and ordinary in narrative content, in every panel bodies react through amplified easily identifiable expressions. In the background of many scenes anonymous people are gesticulating wildly, clearly expressing varying amounts of joy, sadness, frustration, and/or mirth. Rather than relying on quiet tableaux that focus the reader's eye on the main speakers, Tran uses a plethora of relentlessly active figures to populate the scenes. While the members of Tran's immediate family are the most developed characters in the book, this technique illustrates how they live within a world of movement and actions along with others who are busy with their own lives and are markedly uninterested in his family's interaction.

As opposed to many refugee stories that focus sympathy on a particular figure or family, neither Tran nor his family dominate each frame, raising further awareness that they are only one example of the many families and actors inhabiting a dynamic setting. Caroline Kyungah Hong notes that *Vietnamerica*'s subtitle, *A Family's Journey*, suggests that Tran is mapping a singular journey; however, as the memoir takes shape, it ends up tracking multiple generations of actors, charting movement from "South Carolina, Arizona, New York, Florida, Langston, Vungtau, Mytho, Saigon, and back."[32] For most Vietnamese American refugees, refuge was not a one-directional movement from Vietnam to a stable United States but instead involved a variety of movements, first in Vietnam, propelled in no small part by colonialism, capital, and revolution, and then a constant relocation process that persisted upon arrival to the United States. Aesthetically, Tran translates this continuous journey into the graphic image form by creating parallel scenes that are similar but clearly demarcated by different color tones. Each storyteller in the book is provided with a unique color scheme and graphic composition. Through these continuous but distinct perspectives, the reader can viscerally sense that refugee history is a collective effort.[33]

Because families were repeatedly broken apart by the horrors of war and refuge, finding the past requires finding missing family members, plotting and placing them in their absence. Yến Lê Espiritu suggests that Vietnamese American authors must become tellers of ghost stories,[34] and I propose that Tran goes a step further by locating how the social lives of these "ghosts" are manifest in the gestures, rhythms, and places of the living. The sensuous physicality present in every panel of *Vietnamerica* counters the enduring image of the depredated Vietnamese refugee body, an undifferentiated mass hardened through the experience of refuge.

The political importance of identifying somatic resonances can be understood through Thu-hương Nguyễn-võ's call for Vietnamese American artists and scholars to "make the dead tangible," as without this reanimation the war becomes a mere "body count."³⁵ Spurred on by a need to imagine the lives of the missing, Tran's appeal to visual social bodies and historical contexts of Vietnamese families provides a material orientation of wartime experiences without reducing the vitality of these times to instrumental geopolitical desires. This social history necessarily demands that his story straddle multiple national and temporal boundaries, yet this does not eliminate his material and political standing. Whether the title's double entendre is read "Viet in America" or the overlapping of the country names "Vietnam" and "America," his illustrations consistently place the story within political boundaries that compress, violate, and propel the figures in the text.

While there is no doubt that the fecundity and richness of Vietnamese American literature and art has blossomed over the past twenty years, it would be a mistake to think that Vietnamese refugees have only recently been producing artistic renderings of their experiences. Early Vietnamese refugee artistic styles developed quickly upon entry into new lands, and artworks were created even in the refugee camps. Without access to the usual galleries and institutions—and, of course, the disruptions caused by life and death circumstances—the experience of becoming refugees shifted the traditional boundaries between trained and untrained artists in the Vietnamese community. Art classes were taught in some of the camps, and many refugees were able to take up the brush to document their physical and psychological journeys while finding a way to amuse themselves during the long days of detention. As many of these artists had a limited amount of training and expertise, early paintings tend to depict refuge in a direct, dichotomous, and literal manner whereby refugees are fleeing the "evil" Vietnam and reaching toward "freedom"—a word that often appears scrawled over countries such as the United States and France. Despite rather straightforward themes and formal techniques, these earlier artworks display an expert understanding of the global forces that led the refugees to the camps and a reflexive understanding of the images that followed them.

Nguyen Tien Ngoc's *Unreachable Trip* (Figure 1.6) is a strong representation of this type of artwork, communicating how

Figure 1.6 Nguyen Tien Ngoc's *Unreachable Trip*.
Courtesy of UC Irvine Libraries, Southeast Asian Archive,
Veronique Saunier Collection.

the representation of the refugee passage in the media relates to the psychological effects of the journey itself. In his piece, the breakdown of a map symbolizes the blurring of borders for those involved in refuge.

Dominated by jagged lines, this image presents an abstract yet powerful presentation of the difficult and uneven terrain that was traversed during the journey out of Vietnam. Featured prominently is a figure reaching down, across the water, from the top right part of the frame, desperately clawing at the yellow landmass of a converged HK (Hong Kong), Indonesia, and Malaysia. Written underneath these national identifiers is the phrase "boat people," making it clear that the figure in question is a refugee who is seeking asylum in these countries. The jagged lines speak to the distress the figure is experiencing but also mimic the crinkled paper of a well-used map or segments of newspaper print. In the middle of the frame newspaper print takes the shape of some sort of animal, covering about a fifth of the picture, seemingly biting into the middle of the refugee's body. While mainly of indecipherable print, the headline "Vietnamese Boat People Were" is clearly visible, as is the byline "By Paul Rowan," illustrating how biting the representation of the journey was and how the Western coverage of the refugees affected those around the world. As the title of the piece is *Unreachable Trip,* perhaps the journey here was unsuccessful and the anguished face is that of one of an estimated one million refugees who died during this journey and are left out of conventional forms of representation.

By contrast, Hoang Quoc Bien details in Figure 1.7 the conditions of the refugee camps in Hong Kong in a painting titled *Amusement dans le baraquement* (Fun in the Barracks) where despite being successful in their journey, refugees still had to live in a space defined by global forces and contradictions. In the foreground two children play in a makeshift boat; a little girl holds a broom in place of an oar, while a shirtless boy plays with a stick, thread, and some paper fish. Above them three children look down from an upper bunk, leaning over the bars with interested but stoic expressions. While the scene could

Figure 1.7 Hoang Quoc Bien's *Amusement dans la baraquement*. Courtesy of UC Irvine Libraries, Southeast Asian Archive, Veronique Saunier Collection.

suggest joviality, the bunks cut the scene both horizontally and vertically, creating various frames that remind the viewer that the entire scene takes place within a context of imprisonment. The children's bodies are active, in a state of movement; however, the environment around them remains still. Indeed, hard straight lines cover the image, with boxes and crates marked as holding products from both Hong Kong (butter biscuits), and the United States (Sprite and California oranges). The scene thus sits at the intersection of empire, where these foreign products stand in as tools of detention and the force of multinational capital. With the children mimicking the iconic representation of Vietnamese refugees, the painting intimates that the boat people are not going away and offers that the refugee camp is a reproductive space where patterns of life continue despite the desire to eliminate the "problem" that these people pose. Focusing on the children, while a mother nurses a baby in the back of the scene, suggests that a new generation of refugees are being produced during their long detention in Hong Kong. All the while global commercial products continue to enter into this camp, as capital adapts and shapes itself to penetrate this new environment.

What each of these examples shows is that refugees are not only being watched but are also watchers themselves and come to new countries with a repository of information about the historical events they have witnessed and been a part of. Highlighting interpretation, relationality, and global systems, these artists revitalize the iconicity of refugee life by presenting refugee images within differing and individualized spheres of knowledge. By foregrounding processes and structures of value making,[36] these individualized and socially aware figures are shown as meaning-making devices themselves. The interpretive processes, highlighted by refugee narrators, enliven the refugee image so that it does not end as a simple historical symbol but instead is recognized as dense material that can continue to provoke complex questions and answers.

Conclusion: Refugee Encounters

Sara Ahmed argues that "strange encounters" produce the stranger "not as what we fail to recognize, but as that we've already recognized as a 'stranger.'"[37] A stranger allows members of a host community to differentiate themselves from someone or something else, and—to paraphrase Benedict Anderson—to imagine a deep horizontal comradeship with other members in the host nation even though they may never meet. The refugee image, I argue, offers up a certain type of stranger who serves this function while also transforming the viewer into an imagined receiver who evaluates and decides whether the refugee is worthy of entry or not. In other words, the refugee image enables a particular type of imagined community to form through the presumption that they can discern the role of others. Representations of other immigrants can fulfill this function somewhat, but because refugees are admitted on the basis of individual crises, they embody the idea that a sovereign choice is being made. Because nations collectively decide if groups of people are worthy of entry, refugees are central figures in national dramas where benevolence or security can be performed.

Like the stranger, the refugee image is a prepackaged symbol that signifies, at once, a refugee and the failure of a global system. As such, the ways that refugee images are read often have little to do with the refugees themselves but instead express a relation. Sociologist Peter Rose in his 1993 landmark essay "Tempest-Tost: Exile, Ethnicity, and the Politics of Rescue" identifies what he calls "the Madonna of the Refugee Camp" as a trope that is commonly used by relief and resettlement agencies to bring public attention to those caught up in wars and revolutions:

> The specific ethnicity of the emblematic figures may be, and usually is, directly relevant to why and where they are where they are, but in a transcendental sense, it is less significant than their collective condition. With a silent eloquence each singular representation communicates the general pathos of being uprooted and displaced, estranged and afraid.[38]

This passage demonstrates how, in the search for symbolic value, transcendent meaning ends up reifying and stabilizing the content of the image in such a way that bypasses the particularities of the refugees themselves. While I began the chapter mentioning the perils of reading refugee life as a set of distinct crises, there is an equal danger to reading the refugee too collectively, as reading across differing refugee groups can lead to the forgetting of individual experience.

As the production and consumption of the refugee image is historically stable, the refugee image can obscure the specific global forces that produce refugees and flatten out racial and ethnic differences between refugee groups. Rose articulates how interchangeable races and ethnicities become over the passing of time, suggesting that "in the 1970s and 1980s the woman and child of the poignant pieta tended to have Asian or African faces. They were Khmer or Vietnamese; Ethiopian or Mozombiquen. They might well have been El Salvadorian. Today they are Kurdish and Haitian, Albanian and Croatian, Burmese Muslims in Pakistan, and Shiite Iraqis in Saudi Arabia."[39] While there is, of course, a stunning disparity among each group mentioned, presenting them as refugees, which rhetorically groups these bodies in similar situations through similar tropes, subsumes them into a visual category that they all inhabit equally. In this light, the refugee image is part of a racialization process that works on two interrelated registers: first, visually congealing people from all parts of the globe under the category "refugees," and second, creating stark racial differences between incoming and receiving populations by creating this relation. Stuart Hall famously projects race as "a floating signifier" where "race works like a language ... [and] meaning, because it is relational and not essential, can never be finally fixed, but is subject to the constant process of redefinition and appropriation."[40] W.J.T. Mitchell, perhaps unconsciously, builds on this insight by positioning race as a medium itself, where race is "the merging of an ideation complex with individual and collective passions, congealed in forms of totemism, fetishism, and idolatry."[41] And indeed, from this vantage point racialization is not only a significatory system that categorizes bodily characteristics but is also something that works in combination with "the reconfiguration of kinship relations, citizenship status, and spatial (dis)location."[42] It is on this last ground where refugees play a key role in grafting these "secondary" connotations onto visibly racialized populations through rhetorical interplay. That is, the refugee image serves as the technology that merges visual race-based identity and other connotative elements of belonging such as citizenship, foreignness, and nationhood.

Recognizing the symbolic play of the refugee image, what the refugee artist can offer is a glimpse of how the refugee image is read and digested by the refugees themselves—what it means to be an icon that is absorbed into and used by the nation. Centering the interpretive process shifts the refugee image away from serving as a signifier for otherness and recontextualizes these images within a flow of knowledge production. The artist can insert refugee voices into an interpretive dialogue that they were previously not a part of. As such, their efforts are not merely descriptive but instead address the perniciousness of the uneven representative power, performing how the refugee image can become an image of symbolic violence when refugee voices are excluded. Due to the unsavory prejudices that circumscribe the refugee in everyday life, refugee communities are usually eager to leave the image of the powerless refugee behind and, in the process, leave newer refugee populations behind as well. These refugee artists halt these impulses, forcing the distant viewer (and other refugees) to take a second look, demanding that they reread the images through differing aesthetic viewpoints to ensure that refugees themselves are not abstracted into the stable signifier of "the refugee."

2

The Refugee Position

There is something disquieting about the aesthetic qualities that accompany and define the refugee experience. At first, the refugee is produced, detained, and contained at a distance, unable to fully inhabit the nearness necessary for intimate understanding—visible without being knowable. The refugee figure is subsequently asked to transform this isolated position into a phantasmic entity, disappearing from plain sight when incorporated into the national body. From there, the trace of the refugee is circulated around legal categories and political debates shifting away from being an inhabitable subjectivity. This discursive shift rationalizes refugee bodies, camps, and voices as transitory administrative phenomena, enabling a turn away from the refugee experience with the passing of time. Due to the unsavory prejudices that circumscribe the refugee in everyday life, communities are eager to leave the image of the powerless refugee behind. Even authors rarely attempt to intervene in the aestheticization of refugee life; for them, the refugee position is a temporary bureaucratic identity to be overcome. Particularly during the first wave of migration and settlement, writers are more likely to publicly announce their successful arrival in the new land than dwell on their condition as refugee subjects.[1]

However, the aesthetic discourse surrounding the refugee is undergoing a profound transformation, as a number of Southeast Asian American authors are currently embracing the refugee position to document the lingering contradictions that their station entails. These Southeast Asian American authors are producing a body of literature that both invites and critiques dominant culture, elongating the temporality of the refugee condition so that the past is not simply left behind when political designations are removed. By extending the event of the refugee experience, they revisit, interpret, and recontextualize the material pressures that continue to affect their community. Attending to the aesthetics and politics involved in representing the refugee experience reveals the common ground that exists between their own and other refugee communities—a powerful action that ends up calling out the role the U.S. empire continues to play in driving a global history of displacement. This chapter proposes that the new refugee aesthetic style consists of three main characteristics, where authors respond to the demand to explain one's presence, gesture toward *social* identities, and articulate a future for all refugee communities that acknowledges the lasting qualities engendered by the refugee experience. Reflexively attending to both the production and consumption of their journeys, this refugee literature seeks to rewrite the terms of transnational cultural contact that has been rooted in structures of racial dominance and multicultural management.

These Southeast Asian American authors reposition the critical disposition and aesthetic sensibilities found in exilic literature through works that forcefully articulate refugees' unwavering position in the "new" country. As Vinh Nguyen suggests, refuge in the United States is "deeply structured by capitalism, which functions, in conjunction with other forces like race and gender, to fasten refugee subjects to a neoliberal economy that prolongs their search for asylum and settlement."[2] Producing a "state of being and a mode of relationality" that Nguyen coins as "refugeetude," he cogently concludes: "negative experiences become resources for constructing integral subjectivities and modes of aesthetic and social production."[3] Indeed, even when Southeast Asian Americans make significant material and institutional gains in the United States, their national loyalties, economic usefulness, and ethnic affiliations are continually questioned and reviewed. In response, a handful of artist/activists have created an aesthetic style that embraces the complexities that come with their refugee position and write with a dynamism that socially informs readers, roots their community, and critiques U.S. neoliberal empire rather than resting on the literary worth traditionally accorded to the perpetually disoriented exile.

As Southeast Asian American authors must combat a seemingly never-ending stream of uniformed readers who are unaware of the colonial and cultural histories that produce forced dislocation and refugee life, the refugee position becomes an important place to begin to reformulate refugee life. While in his important essay Vinh Nguyen elegantly illuminates the complexities of "refugeetude" as a state of being, this chapter is interested in considering refuge as a *creative position*[4] that makes certain aesthetic interventions possible and becomes something that Southeast Asian America authors can choose to use in order address audience and publishing expectations. Instead of turning to the public and historical locational politics of identity or the claims of subjectivity whereby one denotes who one understands him or herself to be, the focus of this chapter will be the generative possibilities of the refugee position and the outcomes of this strategic aesthetic decision.[5]

The Exile Position and Its Limits

In the academy, the refugee sits just outside the purview of fields that are committed to examining transnational aesthetic forms and formulations, such as postcolonial studies, comparative literature, and Asian American studies. Despite their respective interests in marginal voices, until recently no discipline has claimed this perpetually disenfranchised group as their own object of study, causing the refugee to slip through the cracks of scholarly inquiry.[6] The result of this disciplinary confusion is that the academy ends up mimicking mainstream coverage of the refugee, practicing a distant reportage instead of engaging the subjects and their voices directly. Particularly within humanistic inquiry, academic disciplines and fields favor other marginal positions that promise a more powerful future than this perpetually disenfranchised group. Most notably, the bold and courageous persona of the exile has been an attractive position to explore, for the exile is a commanding figure who can speak for the refugee when the tired huddled masses are politically voiceless. Often a displaced intellectual from the upper class, the exile is skilled in speaking across cultural divisions by appealing to the language of rights, society, and justice. Indeed, when populations remain peripheral—in terms of their linguistic fluency, institutional clout, and civil rights—relying on a few prominent well-educated exilic intellectuals to voice the concerns of the group becomes a practical necessity to make political inroads in the new land.

The exilic author is a familiar figure within the Western literary tradition, with canonical luminaries such as Dante, Voltaire, Victor Hugo, and D. H. Lawrence among the political outsiders who gained productive critical distance by being forced to write outside of their native land. The exile also became a customary part of the academy itself during the World War II era, when American universities blossomed with exiled intellectuals who turned to visiting professor appointments after they ran afoul of their own national governments, transforming the exile from a distant object of study to an embodied, worldly, and critically relevant position. This critical position was codified through exile literature (*exilliteratur*), a group of German-language works of fiction, drama, and critical theory produced by dissident Jewish and communist writers during 1933–1945. Many renowned twentieth-century German intellectuals were considered part of this faction of exiles, including prominent voices of the Frankfurt School. As persecuted people, these writers looked backward to avail pointed and creative criticisms of their former land while concomitantly turning their critical attention toward the larger social structures of ethnocentrism and chauvinistic nationalism, intellectual formations that paved the way for the monstrous behavior that arose during World War II. New positions in foreign countries provided these authors with the opportunity, distance, and urgency to counter the ideological veil that was cast over those who complacently inhabit their homelands in an unreflexive manner.

The work of critic Edward Said has been integral in transforming the exile from a European preoccupation into a worldly position. Drawing from a perspective best embodied by German émigré and theorist Theodor W. Adorno, Said's exile cannot and will not make the adjustment to the new environment—never being at home—preferring to remain outside the mainstream culture as unaccommodating, unco-opted, and resistant. Said's intellectual position was influenced by the disruptive voices and dispositions found in the work of exilic authors such as Joseph Conrad, who find a singular situated sense of self to be unsatisfying. Instead of inhabiting a limited singular position, Said famously states that he feels as if he belongs to "both worlds, without being completely *of* either one or the other."[7] It is important here to pause and recognize that, being a multiple migrant from colonized nations, Said's worlds are not just metaphors or expressions of inner tumult but instead are the psychosocial manifestation of material global determinants. Indeed, his sustained insistence on the interrelationship between discursive, material, and psychological worlds was crucial in generating the political demand for narrative accounts from those whose worlds were traditionally partitioned off from Western intellectual spaces. Yet Said's intellectual project does not simply strive for a hemispheric reversal of fortunes and voices. Nor does it aspire to create more peripheral or in-between positions. As Robert Spencer notes, Said "rejected exile as an attractive *mode de vie* in its own right," with Said himself stating clearly, "Marginality and homelessness are not, in my opinion, to be gloried in; they are to be brought to an end, so that more, and not fewer people, can enjoy what has been for centuries denied the victims of race, class, and gender."[8] In his own case, feeling "out of place" allowed Said the *temporary* and positional opportunity to understand both sides "of the imperial divide"[9] more thoroughly rather than blending the two into one new subjectivity or settling with the de facto marginality of exile.

Said's theorization, then, transforms exile from a passively received subjectivity into a geopolitical position whereby one can practice the skill of separation. Signaling an active and reflexive engagement with migration, the exile subjectivity, in the words of literary critic Timothy Brennan, undergoes a shift from the "locational (being) to the positional (believing or knowing)"[10] as subjects realize their own agency by learning from the material situation in which they now find themselves. Said argues that the exile position involves approaching each new place, land, and idea with vigor, "as if they are about to disappear,"[11] and that the exile should interrogate the roots and connections that posit nation-states as whole entities. Exile, then, becomes a dogged critical practice that involves constantly reviewing and repositioning oneself so as to not be seduced by rote national ideologies or other facile forms of identity generated in countries both old and new. Therefore, what is integral to understand about Said's exile is that while it is a practice constantly seeking intellectual detachment from ruling ideologies, it is still very much of the world and is measured by its engagement with worldly problems.

By this worldly measure Said struggled to embrace, represent, and speak for refugee communities.[12] His exile is an invigorating figure with an unrelenting critical eye; however, the exile's solitariness and indeed Said's own valuation of entities that cultivate the ability to remain separate prove to be obstacle when representing the intimate problems that are endemic to groups of underrepresented people. Said's development of the exile position was a crucial step in theorizing the relationship between the physical experience of displacement and intellectual criticism but comes up short when trying to express the experiences found in a community's social life. The exile position, as theorized by Said, is still a position that can only be occupied by the privileged few. Indeed, while approaching new lands "as if they are about to disappear" is productive as an oppositional critical disposition, it would be a grueling and disheartening practice for those populations that must now stay and make a life in the new land, perhaps over the course of multiple generations. At this level of practical critique, then, there is a need to address the concerns of those who will continue to live in the new land so that distinct refugee voices can be heard now and in the future. While the exile attempts to speak *for* the refugee population, what is missing in this model is a position where one speaks *from* the community. Moving from the temporary position of the out-of-place exile to the socially embodied refugee allows authors to revitalize the nostalgic but powerful critical laments of exilic literature by fully engaging with the new land as the site of present and future critiques.

Briefly surveying the emergence of Vietnamese American literature illustrates how aesthetic innovation parallels the material needs and pressures of the refugee community. The first wave of diasporic Vietnamese literature, spanning the late 1970s and 1980s, is composed of two main bodies of work.[13] One body consists of an abundance of memoirs written in English (or in the tongue of the new land, French, German, and so forth) that were *narratives of invitation* and sought to educate the reader about Vietnameseness and the Vietnamese journey, gesturing toward reconciliation and a mutual understanding. The other body of diasporic Vietnamese writing produced during this period is written in Vietnamese, where *wrath and anger* toward both the old and new lands tore through the literature. This bifurcation of public and private narratives produces a split between simple pedagogical stories that responded to the pragmatic demand to explain oneself and more complex stories that attended to the needs of the burgeoning community and the migrant psyche.

As the population aged and the focus shifted away from the actual migration itself, subsequent generations of Vietnamese American writers repositioned these stories, weaving together the two poles of Vietnamese American literature by moving from individual accounts of survival to the more socially oriented and rooted stories of refugee life. Structural racism, the failures of the American Dream, and intergenerational struggles became central themes in these accounts. Importantly, these stories mapped the common experiences that various Southeast Asian American communities shared, providing the foundation for interethnic understanding and strategic alliances. For example, the demand to explain one's presence began when Southeast

Asian bodies were carefully documented in a series of refugee camps and continued as these migrants settled in the United States. Because of the political valence of the Vietnam War and the suspicion following those who were the physical reminder of this Western imperial failure, Southeast Asian refugees continually had to explain why their bodies had entered these new spaces, creating a persistent dyad that Monique Truong refers to as the "interviewer/respondent relationship."[14] While Southeast Asian Americans, of course, have a wide variety of cultural, political, and historical backgrounds, narratives that engage the refugee experience and map sociopolitical structures such as the interviewer/respondent relationship create common ground that can bond these diverse communities.

From a Place of Refuge to a Refugee Place

Bao Phi, a Vietnamese American poet born in Saigon and raised in southern Minneapolis, has come to embrace the refugee position by attending to the plurality of voices found in his local community. Even though his strong charismatic voice shapes many of his poems, he notes that for him "poetry has always been about more than the self."[15] Belonging to a generation of refugees who have lived in the United States from a young age, he is equipped with the language skills, the cultural capital, and indeed the attentive ear that enable him to tell stories of refugee migration and marginalization in a manner that earlier generations could not. For Phi this responsibility requires honoring the refugee struggle and standing up to people who "assume they can pull shit on my parents because they are economically poor and speak with an accent."[16] Aesthetically, Phi intervenes in the practice of privileging certain voices over others by carefully accounting for why and how each story is going to be told and communicating these authorial pressures back to his audience.

Phi's lyric poem "You Bring Out the Vietnamese in Me" presents the task of articulating a Vietnamese American present without serving up one's community for easy consumption.[17] In the poem he begins with a direct address to the reader:

> *Tôi là một người Vietnamese / Bilingual / Poetry / MC*
> *you want to thank me / không cơ chi*
> *let me take you for a ride / of my refugeography*
> *if your mama could cook you know she'd make a batch of me*
> *nasty catastrophes / ơi trời ơi!/ Fatality / See / Bao Phi*
> *là một nguoi bất lịch sự / Well excuse me*
> *I say one for Asian / Two for American / And three for love*
> *You may say hot like whoa / but I say hot like phở.*
> *Phở real. Phở life. Phở-king Phở-nomenal.*
>
> Because you bring out the Vietnamese in me.[18]

The opening stanza mimics and pays homage to the demands of the interviewer/respondent relationship but colors it with a playfulness of rhyme, rhythm, and language. The first half of the first line "Tôi là một người Vietnamese" is simply stating "I am a Vietnamese person" before shifting to English to add more identities to this initial categorical distinction. This seemingly benign move, however, is a linguistic reversal of the interviewer/respondent structure faced by the earlier Vietnamese refugee generation, whose examination was most often conducted in an unfamiliar language. With Phi's opening salvo the monolingual English reader feels disoriented and estranged, and the easy power dynamic usually established between the interviewer and respondent, subject and inquisitor, is disrupted. The forcefulness of this gesture is solidified through various direct addresses to the reader, in this case not waiting to be asked a question but asserting his multiple identities to his addressee. Mixing colloquial language with directness, the subversiveness of his move is acknowledged later in the stanza, when he states "Bao Phi / là một nguoi bất lịch sự [is a rude person/flippant]." Responding to this charge of impoliteness with "Well excuse me" (which should be considered a less than sincere apology) demonstrates that he is less concerned with speaking truth to power than speaking in a disruptive manner that strives to restage the encounter with a consuming audience.

Phi knows that his ethnic identity is desirable to a readership interested in consuming a multicultural product, and he is savvy in how he reroutes this consuming desire, for despite his strident tone, he carefully leaves cultural touchstones and trails for the nonbilingual audience to pursue. Referring again to the first line, the word "Vietnamese" is not, of course, a Vietnamese language word at all; but rather "Việt" is used to designate the ethnic group. In other words, one would say "Tôi là một người Việt" to identify oneself rather than "Tôi là một người Vietnamese." Adding "Vietnamese" as opposed to "Việt" allows English speakers to infer that Phi is offering up his ethnic heritage, which provides them clues that they can follow for the ride. Throughout the piece he litters the poem with culinary references, in this case riffing on the most recognizable Vietnamese dish, phở. Yet even when approaching this familiar object, he estranges the food from the reader by resituating the accent and in the process disrupting the internal rhyme of his line as he notes "You may say hot like whoa / but I say hot like phở," nodding to the common English-language mispronunciation of the dish as "phoa" and pointing out the diacritical differences produced at this node of cultural convergence. These differences do not make Phi turn away from dialogue, as he remains committed to actively courting the reader with the invitation fully extended in the third line where he offers to take "you for a ride / of my refugeography." Through this gesture Phi clearly embraces the term and persona of the refugee, and when he reads the poem aloud it is clear that the root word here is "refugee" rather than "refuge." The combining form "ography" provides a productive ambiguity, as "ography" denotes both a style of writing and a descriptive science or study, implying a double perspective in which he is studying the refugee experience more broadly—socially—by surveying others as he writes his own tale.

Saymoukda Duangphouxay Vongsay, Lao American poet and the self-proclaimed "Refugenius," takes a less direct approach in addressing the interviewer/respondent relationship in her poem "When Everything Was Everything." Instead of producing an imaginary dialogic scene, she richly layers her poem with images, local names, and languages, creating a dense chronotope of refugee life in Saint Paul, Minnesota. The poem, which consists of fifteen numbered sections, begins:

1. *Food stamps in my pockets. Two dollars' worth of Now n Laters. Green saliva, couldn't swallow quick enough. Standing nervous. Red light on Dale Street. Crossed the bridge over Hwy 94. Trekking back to St. Albans. Candy wrappers clenched tight. Waved goodbye to Tiger Jack.*[19]

Presenting these everyday images of her local community through a series of short, terse lines serves to challenge a reader who is looking to consume this "ethnic experience" whole. The use of street names (Dale Street, Highway 94, and St. Albans) and the allusion to "Tiger Jack" (a legendary street merchant and character in Saint Paul) create a landscape that is undeniably local in flavor and so precise in its references to produce a clear distinction between inside and outside readers.

She continues in a similar vein throughout the piece, literally plotting the spaces of her refugee life in section five, when she lists her various home addresses:

692 North St., St. Paul.
250 Oxford St. North, St. Paul.
308 North St. Albans, St. Paul.
3654 15th Ave. South, Mpls.
1090 York Ave., St. Paul.
130 Bates Ave., St. Paul.[20]

Through these tightly coded details Vongsay creates an impenetrably thick geography, only offering the reader idiosyncratic minutiae of her early life. The outside reader is left trailing behind her emotional journey, scavenging the few details that describe her embodied presence—such as the green saliva that she cannot swallow quick enough and the suggestive disclosure that she is "standing nervous." Through this elusiveness Vongsay refrains from indulging in a peripatetic psychologism by emphasizing instead both her routes and roots via a thick description of a refugee's journey through a local landscape. While feeling out of place is one of the central preoccupations of exile literature, in this poem Vongsay becomes a part of the landscape, functioning as the node through which other people and places are glimpsed.

This sparse opening section is framed by the powerful economic reality of "food stamps in our pocket," foreshadowing the numerous allusions to poverty found in references to expired food, dirty ripped jeans, and the relentless schedule of her father's factory job. Vongsay sprinkles the piece with Lao phrases such as "Pahw mah la, pahw ma la!!" (Dad is home, Dad is home!!)[21] and "Ee la, nyang die yoo baw" (Babygirl, are you okay to walk?)[22] where the reader can contrast intimate, affectionate, and accented social details with the cold realities of Vongsay's socioeconomic station. However, by numbering each section, these intimate details take on the appearance of stand-alone pieces of information about the setting rather than uniquely personal experiences. These episodic sense impressions map and root Vongsay's community in this new physical space through a social realism that resists the "happy ending" of the refugee "melting" into the general population, detailing instead how socioeconomic forces manifest along ethnic lines to continually accent the lives of local refugee people.

In a 2015 interview for the University of Minnesota's Immigrant Stories series, Vongsay states that previously she was trying to piece together her parents' journey in her work. While the difficulty her parents had in communicating their experiences required Vongsay to try to artistically envision what had gone on, she contends that "at some point ... I was trying to imagine too much." This revelation led to a change in her artistic practice, where instead of chasing her parents' distant past she decided that she would "write what I knew"—the local outcomes and enduring qualities of the refugee position.[23]

Positioning the Refugee

In 2006 Yến Lê Espiritu sounded the call for a critical refugee study, which would consider "how and why the term 'refugee'— not as a legal classification, but as an idea—continues to circumscribe American understanding of the Vietnamese, even when Vietnamese in the United States now constitute multiple migrant categories."²⁴ Conventional studies of Southeast Asian refugees in the U.S. academy seek to remedy what is considered to be a problem held in the body and psyche of the refugee subject. Espiritu proposes instead to turn critical attention toward the imperial military interventions and global economic forces that led to widespread Vietnamese displacement. This approach, she argues, counters official narratives of "rescue and liberation," where the rehabilitation of the refugee is needed in order to justify post hoc American policy and turn a military defeat into a "good war."²⁵ As Vietnamese American studies scholars Espiritu, Mimi Thi Nguyen, and Isabelle Thuy Pelaud all contend, this revisionist approach of "we win even when we lose" is an important ideological outlook for the United States to propagate, as the "happy ending" of rescuing the refugee subject provides the justification for subsequent military interventions throughout the world. One of the conclusions that can be drawn from the work of Espiritu, Nguyen, and Pelaud is that narrative structures about Vietnam and Southeast Asian American people are key devices that underwrite American military action. To effectively disrupt this cycle of geopolitical disruption and faux benevolence, though, critical refugee studies must work to refashion the image of the refugee—providing aesthetic critique—so that the refugee is read as a dynamic agent filled with desires, routines, failures, and goals.

Giorgio Agamben famously notes that the existence of the stateless refugee brings into question the fiction that the modern sovereign nation is built on the grounds of rooted citizens. Because of their political precarity, refugees draw attention to the numerous struggles for inclusion that occur within the nation-state on an everyday basis. As their very appearance brings about a disturbance, the state must ideologically externalize refugees, situating them as aberrations and treating them with suspicion and surveillance.²⁶ Southeast Asian American artists such as Phi and Vongsay embody the disruptive energy described by Agamben, refusing to be externalized while calling out the ideological and material violence enacted by the nation-state. This resistance requires affirming one's place and history within the nation-state and also critiquing the ethics behind the state's multicultural management. Often presented as spoken-word pieces, "You Bring Out the Vietnamese in Me" and "When Everything Was Everything" are performed by Phi and Vongsay with a measured intensity and reflective pace that transforms the image of the refugee from a passive subject into an active agent who is not content to settle on a complaint or a problem. This active persona serves to remind the reader of the dynamism and movement in a refugee's life history and acknowledges refugee artists and critics as figures who orchestrate encounters among the state, community, art object, and audience.

The refugee position, then, requires being physically available to and in tune with multiple members of the community while negotiating the institutional space needed to disseminate new ideas and positions. Asian American studies scholar Viet Thanh Nguyen outlines how Southeast Asian refugee critics and authors face a particularly difficult dilemma of speaking for multiple positions, as the transnational nature of the refugee requires representing the country of ethnic origin and other global refugees.[27] Furthermore, Nguyen observes that artists and scholars working in the English- and French-speaking diasporas have a disproportional access to publishing venues when compared to those writing in Vietnamese, so writers and critics of the refugee experience must be reflexively aware of their privilege when deciding what Vietnamese voices are heard on the world stage. Creative and artistic representation is also a complicated matter within the domestic community, as some Southeast Asian American political and social leaders have little interest in left-leaning projects that critique U.S. empire, race relations, and the flow of global capital.[28] Nguyen has argued that as a result of this ideological heterogeneity in the refugee community, if Asian American studies desires to serve the Southeast Asian American refugee population through social justice, this social justice may in fact occlude or even endanger members of the community who have competing goals, desires, and agendas.

I suggest that when engaging this worldly dilemma, refugee literature most often expresses a doggedly rooted position rather than the concerns of a stateless and/or hybrid subject. The situated perspective enables authors to produce intimate and precise portraits of people in need while also providing the sociopolitical knowledge required to identify the structures of dominance that determine who can speak and who cannot. This reading runs counter to Nguyen's assertion that the study of Southeast Asians and refugees can unearth the utopian potential of a country without a nation-state, going so far as to claim that "if [discourse about refugees] critiques nation-states, it must be unsentimental in critiquing refugee aspirations to national belonging, even when those refugees are far from elite."[29] While Nguyen's arguments in the piece are predictably compelling, twinning criticism of the nation-state with a refusal of national belonging ends up repeating the operation of externalizing the refugee position and denies the situated knowledge that forms the centrality of refugee critique.[30] The power of the refugee critique relies on wisdom gleaned by belonging to the nation-state, which, as with George Lukács's proletariat, is drawn from the inside position.[31] Whether this affective and/or political belonging is positive or negative, the knowledge gained from this experience is needed to trouble the very system through which the refugee has been formed.

Precisely because refugee subjects have a heightened awareness of the material perils of existing between states, in practice the literary refugee perspective, whether on the Right or the Left, tends to be wary of claiming indeterminate subjective states like "interstitiality" or "in-betweenness." As the work of Bich Minh Nguyen, Aimee Phan, and Phi (to name just a few) amply demonstrate, using the American insider's voice allows Vietnamese American authors to intimately detail the everyday life and social marginalization that refugees and their descendants continue to face while exhibiting the cultural fluency necessary to appeal to a broad American audience in a strategic manner. The 1.5- and second-generation refugee authors embrace a worldly perspective by exhibiting an intimate knowledge of (forced) relocation and explaining how their subject positions are firmly situated within and have been produced by American state practices.

Furthermore, a rooted voice enables Southeast Asian American authors to showcase their unique and distinct local position to a global readership. Pragmatically, this can be advantageous when courting Western critics and readers who, due to state and linguistic boundaries, have limited access to Southeast Asian writing from Southeast Asia but can feel like they are gaining valuable knowledge of an unfamiliar culture through these American tales. Benedict Anderson surmises in the *New Left Review* that without a unified linguistic block, hefty capitalist allies, or guilt-ridden patronage from their former colonial rulers, Southeast Asian countries will remain minor peripheral players within the global literary marketplace.[32] Attending to the international homologies of the refugee experience thus provides an alternative circuit to highlight and market these ethnically Southeast Asian voices while also speaking to the larger cross-cultural condition of displacement.

As it is not consolidated around a singular ethnic or racial identity, the refugee position can open up a dialogue between cultures and call out the power structures that create displacement and refugee life across the globe. This can be seen when Vietnamese American journalist and short story writer Andrew Lam uses the refugee position to write about the experiences shared between his own and other refugee communities in two of his books, *Perfume Dreams* and *East Eats West*. In *Perfume Dreams* he evokes a shared refugee condition that crosses different cultures and time periods by writing a fanciful letter to a young Albanian refugee he views on television one night. In this piece, "Letter to a Young Refugee," Lam boldly assumes a familiar position vis-à-vis the unknown Albanian refugee: "Listen, even if I know so little about your country's tumultuous history, even if I don't know your name, I think I know what you are going through."[33] While the intimate nature of the address is respectful, the imperative address of "Listen" positions Lam as a wiser older ally. He continues in this pedagogical manner, mapping out the stations and stages of the refugee experience for this Albanian youth who, Lam presupposes, is finding himself bewildered and disoriented. Of course, it is highly improbable that his message will (or is even intended to) reach the Albanian refugee in question, so instead the piece can be read as a reminder to Southeast Asian Americans (and other readers) of the ways refugee history continues to be a part of state practice during the contemporary moment. In addition, the very act of cataloging the refugee experience for a newer refugee community transforms the oftentimes embarrassing narrative of refugee life into an important source of practical knowledge. At the end of the piece Lam sounds the call for other refugee stories to be told, building a useful archive of material, and notes that their experiences "must always be told. And it must, by all means, be heard."[34]

Lam revises this call in his later collection of essays, *East Eats West*, with the piece "Letter to a Young Iraqi Refugee to America." In this piece Lam repositions refugee narratives so they illuminate and critique the continuous global production of refugees, countering the notion that refugee stories are temporary formations that will become obsolete once political designators are removed. Repeating much of the same advice he offered the Albanian refugee in much the same form, in the update "Letter to a Young Iraqi Refugee to America" he delves deeply into the troublesome experience of living as a refugee in the United States when one is a visible reminder of a failed wartime effort—an important commonality shared by both Vietnamese and Iraqi American communities. The advice he offers the young Iraqi refugee is similarly practical and reassuring but also comments on the production, consumption, and use of refugee history noting, "You will find, too, that the American experience in Iraq will, in time, be reconstructed—through books, movies, and songs—into a mythic reality around which the nation flagellates itself and reexamines what now seems its routine loss of innocence. But Iraqis themselves, like the Vietnamese before them, will be relegated to the margin."[35] While Lam's description of the habitual forgetting of the refugee subject is discouraging, his prescient rereading of the refugee experience illustrates how new historical moments can activate the world historical knowledge embedded within Southeast Asian Americans and other ethnic groups who previously held the refugee designation. In sum, Lam's timely gestures resituate the refugee experience from one of fleeting marginalia to a renewable source of wisdom.

While Vietnamese American authors struggle to rewrite an overdetermined history, refugee populations such as the Hmong people must figure out how to write their population into the American consciousness. Mostly invisible to the dominant culture, Hmong American writers face the demand of creating literary works that introduce an underrepresented community to a broad audience and, at the same time, can correct an American history where, in the words of Kao Kalia Yang, "Vietnam was only Vietnamese. How Laos belonged to the Laotians, and the war was only American."[36] The 1.5-generation Yang, who is best known for her 2008 memoir *The Late Homecomer*, explains why she became an author in a personal essay, "To See a Bigger World: The Home and Heart of a Hmong American Writer." In this piece she vividly explains how initially, like many children of her generation, she desired to become a lawyer or doctor to service the many legal needs or the many broken bodies of her newly settled community. This desire, she suggests, stemmed from a way of thinking, produced by history, war, and class, where the Hmong people became "creatures driven by needs, not wants."[37] However, while she was growing up in Saint Paul, Minnesota, life in the United States wounded her in ways that neither doctors nor lawyers could cure, encountering racial abuse and the calls for her to go "home." These taunts produced both a physical and existential quandary for her and other Hmong Americans, as there was no longer a geographical home to return to. The cumulative effect of these experiences produced the question "what does it mean to be Hmong in America? To be Hmong American without the space or place allocated."[38]

In response, Yang takes a similar approach to Vongsay and uses this essay to rigorously map her community's place within the borders of the United States, creating a Hmong American home among the many urban landmarks that populate the Minneapolis–Saint Paul landscape. She speaks of the University Avenue stores around which many Minnesota Hmong people live and patronize, the annual Hmong New Year's events held at the Saint Paul River Center, and the soccer tournaments held in Fort McMurry Field at Como Park, charting and legitimating these places and events where Hmong Americans could feel Hmong and American at the same time—and ultimately at home. Without a geographically present homeland, Yang's generation of Hmong refugees were left to imagine home through stories told by their elders, which were set in a Laos that was solely of the past. In her description of the "HmongLand rising,"[39] Yang plots a home for this generation through the traditional passing down of stories but in this case setting these stories in U.S. places. The work of this refugee writer involves filling this inherited void—repositioning the very idea of home for Hmong Americans—by describing a present that can be recognized and accessed by both present and future generations.

Yang concludes her essay by explaining how writing her own refugee experience led to a greater understanding of communities that share similar cultural predicaments: "I have started to explore other relationships such as how the Hmong story is connected to the Somali diaspora and the ramifications of the political machinations that create populations such as the Yezeti of Iraq—displaced and killed for helping the Americans in the failure of war."[40] With this last move Yang envisions refugee narratives as collectively critiquing the entangled way nation-states dominate domestic migrant communities and embark on more imperial missions abroad that produce new supplies of refugees. By placing different refugee communities in one intellectual constellation, Yang not only finds a home for her own community but also repositions others in a way that calls out American racial acts of war and violence. This mode of refugee literature speaks to and tracks injustice felt throughout the world, turning aesthetic critique into literary statecraft.

Conclusion: The Work of Refugee Literature

Close attention to refugee literature reveals that Southeast Asian American authors often meet the demand to communicate their past by rewriting history in a manner that maps their community's future. Yet these attempts to create future-oriented works are frequently hindered by a readership whose expectations make it difficult for these writers to move their communities' image forward. For instance, Hmong American writing is consistently read with an ethnographic eye that diminishes the literary value of the work. Mai Neng Moua captures this sentiment with her sigh at the beginning of her collection *Bamboo among the Oaks: Contemporary Writing by Hmong Americans:* "How much Hmong history and culture must I provide before we can have a conversation about Hmong literature?"[41] For Moua, the repetitive act of having to present and represent one's past is exhausting, and the burden of educating a perpetually uninformed reader can seem futile. One of the ways refugee authors use literature to address this quandary is by having the pressures involved in telling *their* story foregrounded in the narratives they produce. Specifically, repeating phrases, places, and situations becomes a literary strategy that identifies the weariness of having to return to familiar histories as a constitutive element of refugee creative work.

To further address this weariness, refugee literature frequently embraces a strategic relationship with other aesthetic products, such as cuisine, to underline how the literary marketplace consumes ethnic cultures. Including scenes of food and cooking adds social context that works to thicken the act of reading while offering the cultural particulars necessary to entice a wide number of curious readers. When Southeast Asian American authors take care to contextualize overlapping aesthetic encounters—such as those found in food and writing—their communities are not as easily reducible to a singular cultural essence. In fact, food can even be wielded in a manner that estranges the audience, as is evident in a later stanza of "You Bring Out the Vietnamese in Me" where Phi confronts the reader with a list of Vietnamese foods that are not as easily recognizable to a reader outside the Vietnamese American community as phở. Phi could have easily translated the foods in the lines "the nước mắm, cà phê sữa đá, mangoes and mang cut / mít and coconut, sugar dried strawberries in Đà Lạt"[42] as "fish sauce, Vietnamese iced coffee," and so forth but instead chooses to keep them "foreign" in name. The inclusion of the English words "mangoes," "coconut," and "sugar dried strawberries" teases the English reader while keeping aside an even longer list of edibles that the outside reader is not linguistically and/or culturally fluent enough to consume. Here readers may desire the pleasures of both food and literature, but they are only accorded a partial view, allowing them to indulge in one aesthetic realm at a time—in this case that of literature—disrupting the sense that they are capable of consuming an entire culture.

This act transforms the cross-cultural encounter from being predicated on the completeness and finality promised by aesthetic judgment to the more splintered offering of aesthetic experience. For Phi's initial invitation to the reader, to come for a ride on his refugeography reverses the power dynamic found in the interviewer/respondent relationship, as the reader does not even know where the ride will go. This opening summons, while social, is staged in a way that draws attention to the encounter itself, framing it as a meeting between the art object (the refugeography) and the reader rather than a way to shed light on the entirety of an ethnic world. Philosopher Agnes Heller, for one, considers this practice of creating an aesthetic encounter both useful and ethical, surmising that one approaches an art object with a contemplative but friendly attitude.[43] Taking control of this encounter so he is positioned as an artist rather than a native informant, Phi directs the reader to an experience that forestalls the act of judgment, as one submits oneself to embarking on a ride through the social terrain of refugee life rather than remaining secure in the knowledge offered by a guided tour. Indeed, riding along with the refugee instead of the exile reveals a different perspective for Asian American and comparative work, as the nostalgic critical qualities of exilic literature are rewritten to then activate the new land as the site of present and future social critique.

Literary criticism, as we know it today, was built on the work of European émigrés and exiles such as Leo Spitzer and Erich Auerbach, thinkers who projected a lively air of individual inquiry to work through their received intellectual and cultural attachments. Certainly, one aspect of Adorno's work that Said finds invigorating is his "representation of the intellectual as a permanent exile, dodging both the old and new with equal dexterity."[44] On the other hand, the word "refugee," for Said, "suggest[s] large herds of innocent and bewildered people requiring urgent political assistance," carrying with it none of the "solitude and spirituality" offered by the exile position.[45] This intellectual mapping of forced migrants suggests that the image of the refugee requires an intervention at the level of aesthetics. The conventional forms of representation involve a troubling lack of differentiation and suggest a perpetual weakness that do not attend to the political potential of the refugee position, which in a circular fashion undermines the potential of refugee aesthetic form. Dissolving their past into the promises of the present, this approach only fleetingly glimpses refugee groups before they are absorbed into the nation-state instead of attending to the social conditions and global politics that connect different iterations of refugee life.

In the late twentieth and early twenty-first centuries, the refugee has become no longer a momentary exception but rather a regular feature of the present conjuncture.[46] This requires coming to terms with the refugee no longer being an ephemeral phenomenon and instead a permanent condition visible across nations and continents at all times. In this light, then, I have been arguing that 1.5- and second-generation Southeast Asian American writers are repositioning the way that the refugee is presented. In their paradigm the refugee is no longer characterized by bodily accents, such as those produced in speech, posture, and clothing. Instead, refugee accents are found in the social formations, histories, and national positions that Phi, Vongsay, Lam, Yang, and their fellow authors have felt from a young age. These localized details of refugee life construct a social perspective that draws homologies across different ethnic and racial communities, mapping the lives of those fashioned by global imperial forces.

By extending the temporal coordinates of the refugee position, Southeast Asian American authors are now shaking off the image of undifferentiated herds of innocent and bewildered people while intimately considering the histories of the refugees who have no other choice but to stay. In this light, it is integral to acknowledge that this body of work is coming from a socially fixed and knowledgeable position rather than an unsettled mobile hybridity. The root of Phi's forceful voice is found in his relentless attempts to situate contexts and places, and indeed, it is on this point that thinkers such as Adorno and Said can be helpful in interpreting refugee literature. It is through this socially reflexive aesthetic practice that these Southeast Asian American refugee authors remain unyielding and recalcitrant in their desire to express the contradictions they continue to face in their everyday lives.

3

Refugee Space

Saigon, Vietnam, 2001

Cherry releases the grip around her brother, steadying her trembling feet onto the hot, bright concrete. Lum jumps off his motorbike, leaving his sister to dig her fingernails into their seat, battling vertigo. After inhaling several hot muggy breaths, her eyes finally open.

Identical plots of demarcated land and bleached sidewalks surround her. Wooden beams and smooth stone piles litter the construction site. Men in bright-yellow polo shirts and black jeans crouch along the ground, planting new trees and arranging signs advertising the new housing division. Her gaze resettles on her brother. Lum is beaming.

"What do you think?" he asks.

"It's Orange County," she says.

"No," he says, shaking his head. "It's better."

AIMEE PHAN, THE REEDUCATION OF CHERRY TRUONG

The above is the opening salvo in Aimee Phan's *The Reeducation of Cherry Truong* (2012), a fictional work chronicling the various transnational family crises faced by her Vietnamese American protagonist, Cherry. In this dreamlike sequence both Cherry and the reader are thrown into an unfamiliar iteration of Saigon, where Cherry stumbles through her surprise at finding her previously troubled brother, Lum, thriving in Vietnam, where he works as a developer creating a mimetic version of their native Orange County. The future looks bright for Lum as he builds a U.S.-style development in the Vietnamese nation-state, which, to him, improves on the original by crafting a place for unsettled Vietnamese American refugees abroad.

Phan continues to twist the knife of this provocative geographic juxtaposition at the end of this introductory section, when Cherry is directed toward a sign at the entrance of the development that reads "On a clean yellow billboard, in red block letters, her eyes take a minute to focus [on the words]: The future site of New Little Saigon. . . . The comforts of America, in your true home, Vietnam."[1] The sign's direct address hails a population defined by their mobility with a resting place that promises an elusive combination of comfort and home. This home is a type of Asian America that provides both a new beginning and return for those refugees still uncomfortable in the American landscape while signaling the next stage of geographic expansion for the Vietnamese American community. Trading upon the bifurcated lives and nostalgia embedded in refugees and their descendants, this development constructs a new space by and for Vietnamese Americans in a manner that announces that Asian America itself is a spatial commodity now ripe for export.

Without a clearly defined homeland to reside in, refugees are often imagined as outsiders who are perpetually foreign or, at best, are rewarded for "staying in their place." In this chapter I argue that redefining refugee space, imaginatively, can provide alternatives to these two outcomes. Artists can creatively refashion the refugee's geographic insecurity as flexibility, where space is imagined as an active and malleable force rather than something empty and apolitical. This can be seen in Phan's book, where the combination of Lum's refugee perspective and the replication, commodification, and transposition of an Asian American landscape across national borders creates a unique refugee space that holds the promise of a permanent home. Drawing attention to the deployment of this imaginative force, this chapter also considers how Lum and Phan herself function as refugee mapmakers, whereby refugees and their descendants generate multiple new frontiers by drawing upon the complex relationship to home, space, and movement forged through passages of refuge and periods of adjustment to new lands. Identifying a multiplicity of places, such as the boat, oceans, and refugee camps, as key sites that define the Vietnamese American experience, this mapping of refugee space challenges the boundaries and limits of Vietnam while recognizing that new spaces are possible and indeed inevitable.

This refugee resource is not only the awareness of different spaces but also, importantly, the precarity of space. An aesthetic approach is able to represent refugee space as fraught with tension, and this tension is precisely what requires, or at least gives the opportunity for, refugees to reimagine differing ways of thinking about place, home, and the future. However, we can see in Lum's case how quickly precarity can produce its inverse, where the ability or need to modify spaces is transformed into the refugee's own settler movement, underwritten by the capital-driven creation of "empty space"—where legibility for the refugee depends on ignoring, displacing, and usurping native inhabitants—a process that Evyn Lê Espiritu Gandhi coins as the "refugee settler condition."[2] Indeed, as Quynh Nhu Le argues, despite their somewhat belated arrivals, settler logic can still undergird the relationship between American refugees and the space they inhabit, where they become complicit in perpetuating "settler common sense."[3] With these factors in mind, this chapter explores the types of refugee space that Phan and other portrayals of refugee life present while considering the consequences of someone such as Lum exporting a settler colonial paradigm.

Representing refugee space oftentimes mirrors the public discourse about refugees, where refugee space is characterized as exceptional, marginal, and temporary. But in this chapter, I analyze Phan's book alongside Mohsin Hamid's award-winning novel *Exit West* (2017) to query how these authors provide visions of refugee space that are not limited to exceptional places, such as "the boat" and refugee camps, but instead overflow and shape everyday life. Understanding refugee life as something that unrelentingly transforms everyday places challenges the conventional wisdom that refugee space exists as a place of exception, demonstrating that such space instead troubles sharp imagined divisions between the inside and the outside of nations.

Spaced Out: Asian America and Places of Refuge

The term "Asian America," as opposed to "Asian American," had a minuscule presence in scholarly or creative work until around 2000 but has undergone a surge in Asian American studies academic writing over the past twenty years. Despite the rootedness and place making implied by this spatial terminology, Asian America is a mobile concept that travels quite liberally in intellectual circles, crafting a rather disorienting conceptual history. The term itself has not been theorized specifically but has heretofore been employed abstractly to tie together various social organizations, commodities, or relations. For instance, "Asian America" suggests movement and agency in Daryl Maeda's 2009 cultural history of Asian American activism titled *Chains of Bablyon: The Rise of Asian America*. This movement has a performative quality in Yutian Wong's 2010 monograph *Choreographing Asian America,* where Asian America is something to be controlled and maneuvered. Asian America is consumed and marketed in Martin Manalansan, Anita Mannur, and Robert Ji-Song Ku's 2011 edited collection on Asian American food studies, *Eating Asian America*. The term takes a temporal turn in Minh Zhou and J. V. Gatewood's 2000 multidisciplinary reader *Contemporary Asian America* and Shelly Sang-Hee Lee's *A New History of Asian America*. Erika Lee folds ideas of mobility, performativity, temporality, and futurity into her masterful 2015 comprehensive volume on Asian American history, *The Making of Asian America*.

Despite this rather wide-ranging significatory journey, in all of these works "Asian America" does not refer to an identifiable land-based construction. Rather, as the title of Josephine Lee's *Performing Asian America* (1998) best suggests, Asian America is located and tucked into the bodily actions of Asian Americans.

This formulation of Asian America suggests that Asian American space itself does not exist as an empty container and instead functions as a relation between bodies.[4] Asian America, in both creative writing and academic writing, serves as a relational space-to-come that is posited to represent, locate, and perhaps empower a population. This vision of Asian America, then, follows in the wake of the term "Asian American," contrasting with the common American frontier ideology where people fill "empty space," for in this imagined community the Asian American came first, and Asian America is what follows.

Phan's book departs from this conventional foregrounding of the Asian American by using the physical space of Asian America as a means to build a place for refugee people. While Tina Chen argues that attempting to claim a spot for Asian Americans in the United States has led to an "overcentralization of space as a means to coordinate and prioritize the work of Asian American studies,"[5] refugees have no visible or enduring ethnic coherence and as such are imagined to disappear into the nation-space. Perhaps Phan's unique grounding of Asian America can be read as an attempt to resolve her own contradictory position as both a settled Asian American and a refugee. Refugee spaces are conventionally seen as exceptional, existing only as temporary holding cells to house refugees, and in their artistic renderings usually exist only to be left behind by those who inhabit it. Indeed, refugee narratives commonly map space by describing the circumstances in the home country that prompt the protagonists to leave, chronicling the hardships of the passage, and then examining the physical adjustments involved in living in the host country. The idea of moving on with their lives is often figured as refugees moving from these temporary or embattled spaces toward places that feel qualitatively different from refugee space. In these representative systems, places such as the refugee camp and the boat become engendered with the tangible qualities of refugee experience, places that the refugees must endure until they can embark on the more privileged process of resettlement.

Mohsin Hamid's *Exit West* complicates the division between refugee and settled space. Excising many of the accepted spatial coordinates of the passage by having refugees move to other countries through magical doors, the transnational Asian/Asian American Hamid describes a world where refugee life is a constant condition that affects those both settled and unsettled. This imaginative device removes the distance and clean divide between refugee and nonrefugee space, with refugees themselves forming the immediate physical evidence and outcome of an uneven global system. Viet Thanh Nguyen suggests that this immediacy provides an "interconnected world in which East and West inevitably meet as a consequence of complicated histories of colonization and globalization."[6] I would add that in this particularly spatial mapping of the world system, not only do East and West "meet," but refugee space itself bleeds across the bifurcated lifeworlds of the East/West and North/South divides, revealing the breakdown of these divisions or perhaps revealing the power involved in maintaining this spatial illusion.

In *Exit West*, refugee life defines the contemporary landscape. While the place from which the lead characters, Saeed and Nadia, flee is unnamed, it is described in the book's opening sentence as "a city swollen by refugees,"[7] positioning refugees as *the* physical attribute that shapes the unnamed city. However in the early part of the book the physical and psychic existence of refugees is remarkably prosaic, as the refugees themselves blur into the cityscape. First making their appearance during Saaed and Nadia's morning commute, Hamid relates in a matter-of-fact manner that "refugees had occupied many of the open places in the city, pitching tents in the green belts between roads, erecting lean-tos next to the boundary walls of houses, sleeping rough on the pavements in the margins of streets."[8] In this subtle presentation of refugee life the reader learns nothing about individual refugees, who are glimpsed as masses of people living on the edges of societal life. Like vegetation, they comfortably sit in the backdrop of this part of the story, presented as naturally creeping in and inhabiting spaces that seem open and available. Yet the verb "occupied" signals the forceful changing of the landscape that is already occurring and foreshadows the societal tensions that are to follow. Nevertheless, these people barely register to the protagonists, as in this part of the book (before the protagonists become refugees themselves) Saeed and Nadia seemingly take no notice of their refugee neighbors, although as Hamid dryly notes, "Saeed and Nadia had to be careful when making turns, not to drive over an outstretched arm or a leg."[9] Hamid avoids moralizing about Saeed and Nadia's blindness, however, instead using these asides to build up the structural edifice of the early part of the story, where everyday life and survival take precedence over overt political and social engagement. For the moment, then, the underlying threat of this refugee space remains remote, hidden by and paralleling the actions of the militants who are throwing the city into turmoil, which Saeed and Nadia try to actively ignore as they try to continue with their ordinary routines and courtship.

This ability to maintain everyday life breaks down, as their respective families and businesses, and indeed their growing love for each other, cannot endure the political deterioration of their city. Shortly after the shooting death of Saeed's mother, the pair hires an intermediary to find a magical door that will take them out of the city. Both are tense during the escape; however, their exodus proceeds according to plan. While these doors have a magical realist quality, the movement of refugees is presented as a commonplace fact of life. The doors, curiously, serve to illustrate the banal reality of refugee life; or as Nguyen suggests, they "simply stand in for the reality that refugees will try every door they can to get out."[10] The book was written during a time when dramatic tales of refugees coming from Syria, Iraq, and Myanmar were headlining news programming; however, Hamid's descriptive and matter-of-fact tone presents events as if he is plotting natural physical laws, with refugees flowing through different lands like a river. It follows, then, that instead of allowing his characters extraordinary emotions, Hamid describes the refugee experience with clear declarative statements and a sense of inevitability. Nowhere is this more apparent and devastating than when the couple decides that they must leave the country without Saeed's father. Instead of dwelling on their heartbreak and anguish, Hamid ends the chapter by coolly announcing "but that is the way of things, for when we migrate, we murder from our lives those we leave behind."[11]

The conventionally charged site of the refugee camp is explored only in a slim chapter when Nadine and Saeed go through one of the doors and find themselves in Mykonos; however, it is presented as a rather banal space. Traveling through the door leaves them a little battered and bruised but relatively unscathed as they appear on a beach (a conventional landing place for refugees that they do not avoid even when using the magic doors) and wander into a nearby refugee camp. The camp itself is described mundanely with "many colors and hues but mostly falling within a band of brown that ranged from dark chocolate to milky tea," where "everyone was foreign and so, in a sense, no one was."[12] Drab but by no means exceptional, Hamid relates, "The island was pretty safe, they were told, except when it was not, which made it like most places. Decent people vastly outnumbered dangerous ones, but it was probably best to be in the camp, near other people, after nightfall."[13] Through his flat imagery the camp itself does not hold special significance as a site of refugee life, nor does it carry much weight in the story. The in-between space, usually a prominent site where refugee life is represented vividly, quite literally fades into the background here—rhetorically a shrug of the shoulders—a stop-off as Nadia and Saeed journey toward their ultimate goal of settling into a new home.

It is only when the protagonists themselves enter London as refugees that the book takes a colorful turn. Entering through another magical door, Saeed and Nadia find themselves squatting in a large manor filled with other refugees, whom Hamid makes a point of noting are from Nigeria, Somalia, Myanmar, and Thailand.[14] These real-life locations stand out in contrast to Saeed and Nadia's unnamed homeland, and thus the protagonists emerge as more real and locatable in this moment when they enter the West as refugees. The refugee population here is presented in a lively manner, where food, language, and cultural customs swirl around Nadia and Saeed as they attempt to locate a place for themselves in this multicultural milieu. Much like the refugees in their homeland, in London refugees end up filling the "empty" spaces of the city, but this time Hamid is deliberate in naming the spaces of Hyde Park, Kensington Gardens, and

Chelsea as "hard hit."[15] Mapping the place of the refugees into a Western landscape filled with landmarks that the Anglophone reader can locate, Hamid makes spatial the twin forces of immigrants and immigration in an immediate way. Refugee camps, boats, and processing centers also make immigration spatial but are deliberately hidden from public view, whereas the everyday spaces listed by Hamid are presented in a way that cannot and should not be ignored.

While Hamid's door device and relative disinterest in the refugee camp omit important spatial sites for asylum-seeking refugees, bringing the refugees' usually distant existence into these locatable everyday spaces transforms and indeed threatens the supposed atemporal immutability of these national and global landmarks. The refugees are presented as bleeding into a population and are said to number well over one million. This large number increasingly forces the country around them—and perhaps the world—to notice their presence.[16] Their settlements bring the ire of law enforcement and nativist groups, but these forces are ultimately thwarted by the powerful refugee resistance and indeed by the inevitability of their movements. Following their victory, these industrious refugees begin to physically transform the topography of the land in a more permanent manner, establishing work camps on the outskirts of the city where Saeed and Nadia build housing for themselves and other refugees.

This geographic plotting artfully describes the circuits involved in the creation and maintenance of refugee life by distilling the patterns of rhetoric, policy, and social prejudice that put these people on the move and then drives them to transform the new land they are in. Hamid identifies nativism, land governance, and global commerce as particularly significant forces, with refugees dwelling in the shadow of capital and occupying mansions that belong to absentee homeowners in the West. For Hamid, global capital has brought forth a future filled with refugees where North/South and East/West will comingle with greater frequency and the consequences of colonialism, empire, and war push on the very foundations and limits of prosperous cities in the global North. Writing about a near-future dystopian fictional space distills the template and patterns involved in creating this kind of world, effectively blurring distinctions between real and fictional space as well as refugee and nonrefugee space to create a refugee script that exceeds the emotional plight of the refugees themselves and directs the reader to consider a cosettled present and future where there is no exit from refugee space.

Refugee Mapmaking

From the colonial era to the present day, the ritual of finding, putting bodies in, and naming a map's "empty spaces" is an alluring exercise that can grow cultural identity, empires, and/or capital. The illusion of empty space, of course, prefigures this act, and locating these areas requires a narrative that can envision lands that are open to intervention. This is why, as Edward Said suggests, "the struggle over geography . . . is complex and interesting because it is not only about soldiers and cannons but also about ideas, about forms, about images and imaginings."[17] By analyzing the powerful relationship between geography and knowledge production, Said's work shows that identity, empire, and global capital are themselves ideas that *require* cultural forms to mediate their entry into political and social ideologies. Specifically, maps are uniquely equipped to project the concept of "the world" in its entirety, serving as a remarkably durable form of demarcating boundaries and creating blank spaces, providing a profoundly powerful visual presentation that enables states to assert sovereignty.

In this light, it is worth considering how Aimee Phan's *The Reeducation of Cherry Truong* works as an act of refugee mapmaking and how this mapmaking engages the colonial legacy of dividing up the world's spaces. The transformation of Little Saigon into a new Little Saigon in Vietnam is fraught with unequal global power but at the same time charts new ideas, circuits, and desires about Vietnamese and Vietnamese American life. As Fredric Jameson suggests, the present horizon of the global space requires a sense of abstraction and fantasy,[18] and Lum's New Little Saigon is the manifestation of a utopian desire to export southern California into "empty" spaces on the global map that are ripe for redevelopment. While Southeast Asian American artists, such as Bryan Thao Worra and Mai Der Vang, have used maps of the left-behind country to locate remembrance, longing, or displacement, Phan, on the other hand, uses mapmaking as a remarkably forward-looking device that seizes upon the idea of a "Little Saigon" as a geographic portal that stylizes and adapts space to suit the complex needs of refugee people.

Sau-ling Wong famously introduces the idea of mapmaking into the field of Asian American studies in her analysis of Carlos Bulosan's *America Is in the Heart*. Here Wong methodically reads the number of U.S. spaces that the main character moved through in the book, questioning if this can be considered a record of "Asian American space." This generative engagement identifies a rather unwieldy record of Asian American movement, noting in relation to the "mind-numbing proliferation of place names in parts two to four"[19] of the book:

> Plotting a map for *America Is in the Heart* is, of course, not impossible in the literal sense; given sufficient time and patience, pens of many colors, perhaps transparent overlays to sort out different time periods in Carlos's life, it could be done. But the operation is impossible in the sense that, even if a diagram were made, it would mean little: one could detect neither rhyme nor reason in the crisscrossing lines, see no design in the connect-the-dots-frenzy (not even a retrospectively imposed one such as the first-person point of view would encourage).[20]

The failure of this crude attempt at mapmaking, in other words, is that is does not produce meaning. Or if it does produce meaning it does so in service of mobility rather than delineating space itself. Serving as a decontextualized topographic record, this mapmaking lacks a narrative that allows one to imagine these spaces as Asian American or otherwise. Even though following Bulosan's narrator's journey across the Philippines and the United States is an interesting exercise in charting transnational movement, this kind of mapmaking does not hold the rhetorical or aesthetic power of the "political and juridical" imperial maps created by Europeans where, as William Boelhower suggests, "The function of the first maps was not at all to report a place, but to impose an idea of place on a new continent."[21]

When put into the hands of refugees and refugee agencies, maps can function as important technologies that locate and naturalize the existence of transnational populations that transgress borders. However, it is also true that through repetition and recontextualization these maps are powerful enough to empty or erase humanity through aesthetic abstraction. Transnational Vietnamese American artist Tiffany Chung's 2017 *The Unwanted Population* highlights, through her large pointillist reconstructions of "big data" maps that track refugee populations, the often inhuman ways that refugees are mapped and visualized. On one hand, these maps realign the relative proximity of national borders by attending to the movement of refugees as they travel across the world while illuminating "the utility and bloodlessness of the data sponsored by institutions like the UNHCR and reveal[ing] the ways in which the cartographic, itself an integral part of the colonial enterprise, reproduces knowledge about the other."[22] For, *The Unwanted Population* counterposes these pointillist maps with a video booth that replays gruesome testimony from a survivor who witnessed the killings and endured the rapes that she and numerous other boat people were subject to during the process of refuge, injecting a distressing amount of blood and personal narrative into the viewing process. Utilizing these artistic approaches reveals what Yến Lê Espiritu and Lan Duong describe as "the affected spaces that exist behind, between, and beyond these publicized spaces,"[23] at once gesturing to those who have indeed survived to become refugees and also to the many who died and were left behind during the voyage—who therefore do not appear in conventional narratives, iconic images, or data.

Importantly, the exhibit does not limit itself to the Vietnamese experience, linking the aesthetic and rhetorical commonalities that exist between the Vietnamese refugee and the Syrian refugee crises. By including images and data schemes that seem aesthetically similar, the exhibit demonstrates how maps, data, and images work together to form a comparative system that manages these populations and their movement. In these systems of refugee management, patterns emerge where the maps and images produced by outside agencies, even if they are well meaning, can lull viewers into detaching themselves from the people who live in those coordinates.[24] Chung's re-creations illuminate the map's own aesthetic beauty, drawing the reader in, unencumbered by the messiness of lived experience, and toward space in an almost vertiginous quest for intervention. Indeed, the aesthetic allure of these maps is that they allow the viewer to "compare relations"[25] where not one nation is centered, but identities and places are constructed in contextual spaces. While postcolonial critique has provided a healthy skepticism over the supposed neutrality of maps and other scientific modes of study that propelled projects of empire, Chung's artwork suggests that refugee maps can use the aesthetic allure of cartography to bring into view the ways in which populations, nations, and markets are interrelated—something that capital works hard to obscure.

Of course, maps have an intimate resonance for the Vietnamese American community, playing an important role in the escape from Vietnam, where many of the so-called boat people relied on makeshift maps to guide them toward safety. The refugee's perilous dependence on maps is captured in a passage from *The Reeducation of Cherry Truong* when Cherry's paternal grandfather grumbles, "Do you remember that fisherman's pathetic map? It was so old and tattered. He got it wet several times until Cambodia became Vietnam and then all the countries bled into the China Sea."[26] In this instance, the water-soaked map signified a breakdown of borders and land itself, and suggests that maps are temporary artifacts that change over time and with use. Understanding that nations themselves change in shape and form, refugee mapmaking can highlight this fluidity through figurative or future-oriented maps that use the maps' aesthetic allure to train readers/viewers into seeing new boundaries, possibilities, and even different kinds of "empty spaces."

Traditionally, though, Little Saigons are conceived of as anything but empty and instead are marked as thick spaces where bodies, buildings, and social organizations are formed in relation to each other. When recently diasporic people migrate transnationally, microversions of cityscapes usually become the new home to the incoming population, characterized by their bustling overlap of businesses, restaurants, and people. These cityscapes are marked by their denseness, commercial exchange, language, and food. This differs greatly from Phan's placid imaginative New Little Saigon settlement, a suburban oasis of neatly "demarcated land and bleached sidewalks,"[27] a pristine, organized, and indeed utopic American development waiting to be occupied by overseas returnees. Relying less on the haphazard confluence of businesses, restaurants, and chaotic density of the city, these suburban forms promise a seemingly unlimited supply of empty reproduceable space.

This mode of spatially expanding "Vietnamese America" should reanimate debates about the political and economic influence of the Vietnamese American community on the rest of the world. Indeed, over the past twenty years Vietnamese city planners in Vietnam have been looking for ways to modernize southern Saigon, and architects are turning to contemporary Vietnamese American ethnic enclaves for inspiration. This drive is captured in Seth Mydans's *New York Times* article on the transformation of Ho Chi Minh City, where he notes that "the fresh face of Saigon South is . . . uncannily similar to the version of a modern Vietnam that was created by refugees as Little Saigon in Southern California. In its newer districts, it might be said, big Saigon is being transformed into a big Little Saigon."[28] In this transnational light, Asian America is exceeding its purely academic and literary usage and stands as an imaginative symbol of modernity filled with possibilities—particularly economic ones. Over the past twenty years, Asian Americans en masse have been able to trade off of this aura of modernity overseas, playing a large role in the promotion and development of transnational cultural industries such as K-pop and inventive cuisines. The Asian American economic influence in Asia is certainly not new, as financial remittances and market investments have continually shaped the culture of the left-behind land or that of their ancestors. However, this shift whereby cloistered communities are carved out in less developed economies, both physically and aesthetically, carries with it the scent of settler colonial land grabs, and this reordering of space can be a driver of American capitalist imperialism in the present. In this sense, ethnic ties become tools to exploit underdeveloped lands, and this positions the United States as the utopic spatial model of Asia's future.

Yet for refugees themselves, an American "spatial modernity" can complicate their relationship to home, as geography and the blurring of borders haunt all the characters in *The Reeducation of Cherry Truong*. The book's plot is driven by Cherry's wanderlust and her testing of different spatial grounds, where her movement across various places of Vietnamese refugee life—such as the refugee camp in Malaysia, Cherry's parents' house in Orange County, the nail salon that Cherry grew up in, Cherry's grandparents' place in Vietnam, and her uncle's family home in Paris—creates a plurality of diasporic coordinates that challenge the first generation's binary existence, which oscillates between the memories of their left-behind country's past and the practical realities of the present-day land. Spanning over two decades of Vietnamese refugee life (1979–2002), the book presents its story in pieces, mapping the refugee dispersal itself by tracking the stories of multiple family members. This multiperspective narrative tells a refugee story defined not just by the war or any particular injustice but instead by the snaking paths that Vietnamese people have made around the world.

Characters in the book are never quite settled, feeling slightly out of place no matter where they find themselves. In particular, a sense of transient uneasiness colors life of the first generation of Vietnamese Americans in Orange County, with Cherry's grandmother symbolizing the refugee's difficulty "fitting in" or "settling down," moving from house to house as she lives with a circuit of relatives for only a few months at any given time. Further, the trauma of refugee camp life bleeds into the new unfamiliar U.S. space with Cherry's mother relating that in the refugee camp "we had no protection," which drives her to lock the doors of their new house by rigging toy bell alarms on the front door to secure the home while Cherry's father is working.

Despite this desire to keep the family safe, secure, and locked away in their homes, the parents' geographic insecurity and desire for stability create a stifling and inhabitable place for Cherry and her brother, as each child is driven to travel to spaces outside of the United States. Lum is actively sent away by the family to Vietnam in an attempt to get him out of the trouble that constantly follows him in Orange County, hoping that removing him from the U.S. space will settle him down. Sending him back to Vietnam seems effective, as he is successful in finding meaningful employment, gets married, and starts a family. This version of success, however, is less a matter of him finding familiar values or a "true home" in Vietnam and more a matter of his refugee and American consciousness having a particular value there that gives him a unique opportunity and the necessary authenticity to construct his New Little Saigon. As Long Bui argues, "he is a refugee who 'escaped' the small enclosure of his family and the provincialism of the Vietnamese American community to reeducate himself in the bourgeois ways of global capital . . . and reeducate South Vietnamese people on capitalism."[29] Lum's reformation, then, turns on his ability to enact a settler colonial transformation of "empty" land and convince others that this is their future. This future is the invention of a specific model of Orange County that empties out space to build an interchangeable and transportable U.S.-style community.

As a bright second-generation rule-abiding student, it is expected that Cherry would be the most rooted and comfortable at home; however, she defers her medical entrance to the nearby University of California, Irvine, and instead searches for the past by visiting different spaces, traveling to Paris and Vietnam, in part to leave the stultifying future offered by Orange County behind. Near the end of the book when Cherry travels to her brother Lum's home in Vietnam's New Little Saigon, it is striking how their late-night walk is described in a positive and even homey manner, particularly when contrasted with her initial disorientation in encountering the development. Slowly she is adapting to this new iteration of Orange County, recognizing it as an Asian American space:

> Though they are the only occupants on the block, the gaslight streetlamps cast a warm glow on the sidewalk and fresh asphalt—so much energy burning for only one house. If it weren't for the humidity, Cherry could easily imagine herself in Orange County. She watches the long shadows they create, and attempts to step on her own. . . . They leisurely walk round another block, listening for some time only to their footsteps. Cherry feels like she can walk this cul-de-sac and never get tired.[30]

In this leisurely moment Cherry's body finally finds comfort in this mimetic land, feeling *almost* at home in the cocoon-like development that surrounds her and her brother. Just about being able to step on her shadow, she seems close to finding a match for herself—a whole—but in the meantime she is content to loop around in circles, amusing herself in this cul-de-sac with only the rhythmic pace of their footsteps marking their place in the physical world. Never quite able to fully inhabit this space, however, Cherry's thoughtful character ultimately moves on from this development and turns away from the future carved out by Lum privileging her sense of mobility over the engineered rhythms of this potential "home."

While most tales of refuge begin on a boat, this story ends on one, as Cherry drifts, as a tourist, on a fishing junk in Vietnam's Ha Long Bay with her Parisian cousins. The book concludes with a group of children, an even newer Vietnamese generation, dropping into the water a number of letters that were given to Cherry by her grandmother. Cherry literally treads water as they fall, watching helplessly as these intimate family documents sink to the bottom of the ocean. The drowning of these letters suggests that her traveling through different spaces cannot and will not allow her to access the past, and instead Cherry must drift toward her future while the letters and memories of her ancestors are laid to rest in their native Vietnam.

Conclusion: The Future of Asian America

The relationship between refugees and the spaces they inhabit is often fraught with tension. Phan's imaginative foray engages with this geographic insecurity by proposing another future for Asian American space abroad, demonstrating how refugees will continue to transform the landscape of both the present and the future. Similarly, Mohsin Hamid's *Exit West* shows how refugees, as a population, now constitute a force that will continue to alter spaces, ideas, and lands—offering an alternative for refugees who have been led to believe they have to choose between expressing unending gratitude or accepting their own disenfranchisement. The authors, each in their own way, suggest that the world needs to understand that this new enduring reality of refugee life will shape the future and that reimagining refugee space is an opportunity to relocate refugees on the map.

Representing refugee space allows for a critical reexamination of the act of dwelling for both refugees and others, illuminating the intertwined relationship between physical orientation and ideas about space. Defining space often involves both a land grab and a set of political ideals that seek to circumscribe the present and the future, or as Kandice Chuh opines, "Territoriality literalizes nation, lending to it a palpability that contributes to its sense of inevitability."[31] As a community informed by exile and refuge, Vietnamese American artists and architects have the opportunity to imagine Asian American territory, transnationally, in ways that avoid succumbing to the inevitability of manifest destiny. For instance, Lum's development promises a unique place that can cure the nostalgia that has wracked the first generation of Vietnamese refugees and also provide a "better home" for wayward second-generation Vietnamese Americans such as Lum himself. While Lum could be considered a crass businessman, he is also leveraging one of the greatest skills he has: the ability to transform the ideas of "Vietnam" and "Asian America" into a future-oriented refugee space through his imagination and acumen. Refugees problematize national myths as they disrupt the idea of a natural relationship between land, place, and home, a point that Hamid illuminates in his breaking down of "a specialized logic that holds a discretely and naturally distinct 'here' and 'there.'"[32] His story recognizes that refugee space is interwoven with the everyday spaces of nation-states—presenting refugee space as ordinary rather than exceptional. For Hamid, refugee space is good to think with, as it reconsiders accepted cultural formations and social limits, reminding the reader that new spaces are possible and indeed inevitable.

However, *The Reeducation of Cherry Truong* also demonstrates that when creating new spaces, the refugee can become a settler who transforms space, markets its aura, and then exports this intervention as a commodity. On the surface, what is offered to the potential inhabitants of Lum's development is not the complexity of an Asian America to come or a relational mode of being but rather a simple one-to-one physical reinvention of an overseas local formation. Yet Phan hints at the sleight of hand involved in Lum's transnational re-placing, warning the reader that "the space looks idyllic, but now business can commence" and disclosing that the different housing options offered in Lum's development are named "the Magnolia, the Westminster, the Bolsa, and the Brookhurst"[33]—all spatial references to Orange County's Little Saigon. The gated community that Lum offers consists of a series of interchangeable houses, but naming them after the main thoroughfares of Little Saigon (Magnolia, Bolsa, and Brookhurst) as well as the city that encompasses this district (Westminster) differentiates and brands his development by transforming recognizable Asian American coordinates into transnational spatial signifiers. While Lum's "Orange County," packaged for export, relies on the names of places that define Little Saigon, the suburban housing development does not accurately match all of the kinds of businesses and housing that comprise the area. The idea that Orange County is a series of identical and interchangeable plots of land could not be further from the truth, as whether in Westminster, Santa Ana, Newport Beach, Costa Mesa, or Tustin the area contains a extraordinary variety of places, classes, and people. In presenting this scene at the beginning of her book, Phan seems to ask the question: what kind of Orange County or Asian America is ready for export? For positing and selling this idea of "Orange County" and, by extension, Asian America as a reproducible interchangeable space empties "Orange County" of its referential variety and tension.

When Cherry initially sees Lum's uncanny New Little Saigon, she describes it as looking like their home back in "Newport

Lake," but in reality there is no Newport Lake in Orange County. Indeed, Phan admits that she invented this place as an amalgamation of Newport Beach and Lake Forest,[34] two communities known for their planned gated communities that sit considerably outside of Westminster's Little Saigon. This "Orange County," then, is a discursively created "empty space" that uses the markings of Little Saigon to perform the utopian (and dystopian) fantasy of settler colonialism in Vietnam. These settler colonial acts infect the newly actualized space of Asian America with an American frontier ideology that positions Vietnamese space as premodern and awaiting transformation. As Hamid's book lays out, refugees have been transforming space and will continue to do so. In this light, it is no longer enough to think of Asian America purely as an intersubjective form. Rather, Phan's story shows that thinking and dreaming Asian America spatially is necessary, as the battle has begun to determine if Asian America can hold any utopian outcome in its own right or if it will serve as just another commodified settler incursion of America in Asia.

4

The Refugee Personality

At best refugees have voices, but up until now they have never had personalities. There certainly has never been a refugee with a public presence quite like Viet Thanh Nguyen's, and in concert with the "bad refugee" protagonist presented in his Pulitzer Prize–winning novel *The Sympathizer,* he has changed not only the face of refugees but also the ways they are known to talk, act, and write. The force of Nguyen's public personality provides an important counterpoint to the nameless masses conventionally found in portrayals of refugees, while the critical and commercial success of his novel suggests that refugee stories can appeal to U.S. readers when told creatively and through innovative formal techniques. Leveraging the access that his Pulitzer Prize has garnered, he has toured the book tirelessly to educate readers, reviewers, editors, and interviewers about the literary and ethical choices available to refugee artists. And indeed, Nguyen's position as a visible Vietnamese American refugee author and academic provides him with the cultural capital necessary to speak brazenly and effectively during his promotional tours about the ongoing legacy of the American interventionist war in Vietnam. Through his consistent foregrounding of the refugee position, Nguyen has argued that Southeast Asian American literature is particularly important during the present moment, as these refugees and their descendants can provide necessary and trenchant critiques of empire, neoliberal governance, and militarism.

Nguyen's critical perspective has been developed through a sustained academic engagement with Asian American and postcolonial studies, and this academic approach informs both his fiction writing and literary persona. Previous to his Pulitzer Prize win, Nguyen was best known for his position as a professor of English, comparative literature, and American studies and ethnicity at the University of Southern California, where he has served as a leading figure in Southeast Asian American and, more broadly, Asian American studies.[1] Intimately concerned throughout his scholarly oeuvre with the ways that Asian American writers represent themselves and are represented, Nguyen is well aware of the pitfalls that an Asian American and/or refugee text can encounter when it is delivered to the literary marketplace. For him, the stakes of creating this body of work are high, as in his own words "Asian American literature literarily embodies the contradictions, conflicts, and potential future options of Asian American culture."[2] Yet as he argues most thoroughly in his first academic book *Race and Resistance: Literature and Politics in Asian America*, once an Asian American literary work is put into circulation, the political significance of the book is shaped as much from the "biases and priorities" of critics as from the text itself.[3]

With this holistic view of Asian American literature in mind, I propose that Nguyen's professorial record, his public persona, and his unique celebrity must be analyzed in concert with his literary creation when assessing the impact that *The Sympathizer* has made as both a text and object. Or to phrase it slightly differently, in this chapter I consider *The Sympathizer*, its massive publicity tour, and the ways Nguyen frames the book to be a unitary performative piece. Approaching this entire enterprise as the object of study spotlights many of the contradictions that refugee and Asian American authors face and the tactics they deploy when crafting their texts for consumption in the literary marketplace. For instance, in his fiction Nguyen steadfastly refuses to pander to his non-Vietnamese readers by "translat[ing]" cultural elements of the text, and he is not willing to tailor his work toward a niche audience, writing instead as "if [he] had all the privilege of a majority writer."[4] Yet in the selling and promoting of the book, he is frequently presented as a "Vietnamese" author who can present a unique take on—or "the other side"—of the war. In these moments he is tasked with presenting this take while also appealing to and selling the book to a predominantly white American audience who already has a deeply entrenched impression of what the Vietnam War was about and means. Faced with this challenge, instead of assuming the role of the cultural translator, Nguyen takes on the authority of a professor, and when discussing the novel he expertly steers the discussions toward the relational ethics behind war, the enduring qualities of the refugee condition, and the process of writing as a Vietnamese American. This professorial ease that he has developed in guiding these debates provides him with the dexterity to firmly set the parameters for these dialogues, taking these opportunities to present nuanced and at times contrary versions of events that have become central to the American consciousness. Selling the book, then, gives Nguyen the educator an opportunity to assume the role of a public intellectual in the sense proposed by Edward Said: Nguyen uses his platform to actively advance broad humanitarian concerns of freedom and knowledge while at times upsetting the status quo.[5]

Considering the breadth, richness, and scope of Vietnamese American writing in the twenty-first century, it is worth contemplating why and how Nguyen's debut novel has resonated so profoundly to a broad audience while other Vietnamese American literary work remains read primarily within Asian American literary circles. His entry into the literary marketplace has occurred during a particularly fertile and active period for Vietnamese American literature, when new writers such as Ocean Vuong, GB Tran, and Thi Bui are using a wide array of literary forms to build upon the ground established by authors such as Aimee Phan, Bao Phi, Bich Minh Nguyen, Linh Dinh, and Lan Cao. Before the rise of *The Sympathizer,* Monique Truong's 2003 *The Book of Salt*—an inventive, worldly, and profoundly literary work about a queer colonial Vietnamese chef living in Paris—was the most well-received Vietnamese American text among critics and in college curricula. While it won a handful of awards, including the PEN literary prize, it certainly did not acquire the crossover appeal of Nguyen's novel. Conversely, Le Ly Hayslip's 1989 memoir *When Heaven and Earth Changed Places: A Vietnamese Woman's Journey from War to Peace* gained widespread notoriety when Oliver Stone adapted it for his 1993 film *Heaven and Earth;* however, the book has not endured as a literary text and is all but unread in university classrooms. Perhaps this is because Hayslip's book was read by the mainstream press simply as a "lesson" for the United States about the perils of war, told by a woman who had produced a "searing and human account,"[6] instead of something with a uniquely Vietnamese voice and personality. Indeed, the *Washington Post*'s proclamation that "No one who reads [*When Heaven and Earth Changed Places*] will ever be able to think about the Vietnam War in quite the same way again" demonstrates how individual refugee voices become obscured when books are read as a lesson about the Vietnam War, which oftentimes involves reading a refugee story as a general human one. On the one hand, Truong's work may have been too literary and esoteric to garner a poignant response from the broader American reading public, but because Hayslip's book was marketed as universal in its scope, the specificity of her voice did not endure long past the historical moment that it was written in.[7]

Nguyen's take on the spy novel produces a marketable war-and-refugee story that has the right auratic mix of universality and specificity to engage both critical and popular audiences. Creating a spy novel that offers Asian American critique challenges or perhaps even reconfigures the boundaries of a genre with a long history of producing and reinforcing pernicious racist and sexist stereotypes.[8] Nguyen's multiethnic and transnational narrator in particular upsets the orderly racial and national structures that the spy novel's stereotypes typically rely on. Yet as an alcohol-fueled womanizing bachelor with the flashy and suave demeanor of Ian Fleming's James Bond, the narrator provides comfort to the regular reader of spy fiction by fulfilling characteristics common to this genre's male protagonists. As Kathryn Cope suggests, underneath this veneer is a character that also has much in common with the spies found in the novels of Graham Greene and John le Carré: "world-weary agents who have become morally exhausted by the corruption they have witnessed on both sides."[9] Instead of resting on the frustrations of living in an overly bureaucratized world, however, Nguyen's book reminds the reader that navigating social and political relations in a global network of competing interests requires more than good intentions and instead requires an active intelligence, which indeed is a fundamental moral lesson also offered by *The Sympathizer*'s ghostly influence, Greene's *The Quiet American*. This brand of active intelligence is driven by self-reflexivity and rigorous introspection about the position(s) one holds in the world, which not coincidentally are the attributes that educators in the humanistic disciplines seek to develop in readers and students in order to produce social change. As Asian American studies scholar Daniel Kim has suggested, the book is in many ways Asian American Studies 101, yet to those unaware of the debates central to this ethnic studies field, the spy novel allows Nguyen to present the narrator as working through seemingly "universal" quandaries.[10] In this light, one could say that Nguyen performs a work of espionage himself, gaining access to a wide audience by publicly presenting himself as just a prize-winning author while clandestinely still doing the work of an ethnic studies professor and educator.

Studying the Literary Marketplace

Along with the meteoric rise of *The Sympathizer*, an unprecedented level of celebrity has been afforded to Nguyen himself, and his status as a highly visible Asian American author has presented him with the unique opportunity to play a large role in positioning how his book is read. His literary and intellectual approach cuts against the grain of conventional and iconic immigrant narratives, and among many other honors this approach has provided him with the platform to write for the *New York Times*, serve as a keynote speaker at the national convention for the Modern Language Association, and be interviewed by Tavis Smiley, Charlie Rose, Seth Meyers, and Terry Gross. Yet in many ways this brush with celebrity is not Nguyen's alone, for the unprecedented visibility he has garnered influences the reception of Asian, Asian American, and refugee literature writ large. Read by interviewers as a Vietnamese American and oftentimes as the live correspondent for the missing Vietnamese voice from the Vietnam War, he addresses these assumptions in a way that frames potential readings of *The Sympathizer* but also impacts the marketability and aesthetic position of other Vietnamese Americans' literary products. In this light, Nguyen's paratextual performances can be read as interpretations of and interventions in the marketing and reading practices that determine the place of Vietnamese, Vietnamese American, refugee, and Asian American entries in the literary marketplace, particularly when these works are assumed to bring the voice of "the other."

Anticipating these types of pressures, or perhaps opportunities, the act of consuming and framing images of your own ethnic group is a key storyline in *The Sympathizer*. At one point the narrator is tasked with reviewing a script for an *Apocalypse Now*-type Hollywood film about the Vietnam War called *The Hamlet*. The narrator's primary critique is that there are no speaking parts for Vietnamese characters, and even once they are (reluctantly) added to the script, the narrator travels to the set to discover that Vietnamese roles are not being played by Vietnamese actors. The animosity that develops between the narrator and the director over the representation of Vietnamese people in this somewhat farcical section reaches a boiling point when the narrator is severely injured on set by a misfiring special effect that later is implied to have been an "accident" coordinated by the director in order to rid himself of the narrator's meddling presence. Even though this episode is presented in a darkly humorous manner—with a white American director filming a movie about U.S. heroism and benevolence during the Vietnam War nearly killing a Vietnamese person in the process—the grave consequences involved in the interlocking of representation and war are no joke.[11] Identifying these reflexive moments as central components of Nguyen's narrative performance, Karl

Ashoka Britto insists that "at its core, *The Sympathizer* is about power and representation, about stories that function to justify torture and murder, and about words that make abstract the bodies of people whose lives have been shattered by colonialism and war."[12] Additionally, when taking into account Nguyen's academic interest in the ways that popular stories shape national memories and wartime projects, one can see how *The Sympathizer* is positioned as a postmodern performance piece that lays out the stakes of its own existence. Directly engaging the conversation regarding literary representation, Nguyen uses a critical psychosocial reflexivity to both document and counter stories that "make abstract the bodies of people whose lives have been shattered by colonialism and war."

Nguyen's *Race and Resistance* (2002) contends that the conventional criticism of Asian American literature revolves around a fundamental misreading, as this body of work is usually assessed along the axis of accommodation or resistance. Arguing that this approach reflects more the desires and politics of the critics themselves than the actual contents of literary works, Nguyen calls for readings that consider the "ideological heterogeneity" of the Asian American body politic.[13] This concern over ideological heterogeneity is driven by the recognition that whoever frames a binary choice (for or against, accommodation or resistance, etc.) holds great power in defining the terms and indeed the very subject that is to be interpreted. Retrospectively, we can see this argument as the beginning of his ongoing critique of the U.S.-centric master narratives that surround the Vietnam War, as denying the Asian American community's ideological heterogeneity is analogous to the carelessness and danger involved in broadly grouping together all elements of "the Vietnamese side" in order to form a rhetorically cohesive oppositional other.

The task of writing stories that counter these U.S.-centric narratives is addressed in a 2006 essay titled "Speak of the Dead, Speak of Viet Nam: The Ethics and Aesthetics of Minority Discourse," where Nguyen argues that the act of speaking of the dead is an ethical obligation of the refugee writer, even if this ends up "perpetuat[ing] the haunting, rather than quell[ing] it."[14] This *act* of speaking of the dead, which is potentially disturbing, turns attention to the speaker/storyteller, who is thus required to claim responsibility for the work rather than hiding behind esoteric ideas about aesthetic play or poetic license.[15] This responsibility is evident in Nguyen's dedication to acknowledging while not altogether embodying the plurality of voices that underwrite both his literary and academic endeavors. In this light, the essay could be read as a challenge to himself to write in a way that rectifies, or at least acknowledges, the conventional rhetorical limits that both academic and creative genres face. And while a comprehensive perspective may be impossible, a comprehensive performance is at least glimpsed through his impressive achievement of publishing three works in three different genres in three consecutive years.[16] This combination of academic and literary success provides Nguyen with the generic flexibility and public profile to consistently reinterpret images of himself and his work, an introspective and strategic process described by Sarah Brouillette whereby "literary production is influenced by the development of authorship as a profession and by the process through which writers consume images of themselves and reinterpret those images in order to negotiate and circulate different ones."[17] The need for this reflexive interpretational act is acknowledged in his second academic monograph, *Nothing Ever Dies: Vietnam and the Memory of War* (2016), where he suggests that the minority writer, while often speaking on behalf of the victim, must also have a sophisticated sense of her or his own position, specifically the ability to both heal and harm. Underwriting his admonition that one should not claim the simplistic position of victimhood is thus a recognition that writing from a minoritarian perspective should involve an author presenting to the reader a plurality of voices that often contradict each other in their goals, desires, and methods.

In his academic criticism Nguyen examines the historical interplay of aesthetics and politics, focusing on how literary tastes, exotic representational histories, and the battle over wartime memory shape the representations and representational power of Vietnamese people across the globe. This scholarly perspective allows Nguyen, in interviews, to draw a straight line between what it was like to live as a Vietnamese person in the United States during the refugee era and the material and representational challenges that Vietnamese Americans face today. When addressing readers, editors, and interviewers, he takes on the dual role of pedagogue and artiste by providing an expansive cultural history lesson that focuses attention on the decisions he makes as an author while surreptitiously moving the discussion around like a scholar. While he could rest on alerting readers to pernicious, stereotypical representations of the Vietnamese and Vietnamese American experience, his choice to guide interviews toward his own creative choices illustrates the parallels that exist between both himself and *The Sympathizer*'s protagonist, showing how they are equally thoughtful, minoritarian, and dangerous. Blurring the divide between his fictional account of a Vietnamese American spy and his own challenges writing as a Vietnamese American author, this continuity between the diegetic world and Nguyen's life eschews the idea that they are both merely victims and instead presents two different men who are complicated and indeed unique. When Nguyen frequently turns interview time to his own struggles and failure to find *his* voice, in many ways he is drawing attention to the process of trying on different expressive forms that will persuade the reader to engage larger social issues. Speaking out about the representational choices and contextual struggles available to a person in his position demonstrates how Vietnamese writers can transform the contradictions and violence embedded in their own performance of ethnicity into a political project of remembrance where they speak as and for a number of heterogeneous voices.

In a 2016 book chapter titled "What Is Vietnamese American Literature?" Nguyen identifies writing about the war and refugees as the central challenge that Vietnamese American authors face. However, this challenge is a matter of not only representing what are undoubtedly traumatic events but also developing a critical position that can call out and decenter the U.S. position in this international conflict. As Nguyen explains, there is an ontological riddle woven into Vietnamese American critique: "On the one hand, this literature speaks of the war and the terrible things that happened to the Vietnamese and that the Americans did in the name of supposedly defending freedom. On the other hand, the existence of Vietnamese American literature proves that America, in the end, is a beneficent country that ultimately fulfilled its promise of freedom."[18] Because there is a persistent belief that American authors are supposed to speak up and speak out, telling *their* story in real time, Nguyen argues that it is extremely difficult for the immigrants, refugees, exiles, and strangers, who often come to the United States speaking a different language than the dominant one found in the country that they are entering, to tell their story with the requisite amount of urgency and force to immediately intervene in the common national discourse. Since the first wave of migrants are often only heard in their own ethnic enclave communities, they must wait until the second generation can speak for the first generation if they are to be heard by the wider American public,[19] by which time there already exists a large body of non–Vietnamese American writing and cultural production about the war. This puts the second-generation author behind in regard to temporality and archival authority. Further, even when second-generation Vietnamese American authors may want to write about something else, they know that speaking to their elders' history is expected from their community (and perhaps from their own sense of social justice), and they understand that writing about this history is also rewarded in the literary marketplace.[20] Speaking for their community does accrue these authors some cultural and economic capital, but as Nguyen points out, "in an economy of narrative scarcity and inequality, the ones with the real power are the outsiders to the ethnic community who already have so many more stories and who are the real insiders: the readers, agents, editors, publishers, reviewers, and critics who demand that things be translated to them."[21] This economic and aesthetic structure mirrors the cultural myth of the perpetual foreigner whereby in order to gain access to the literary marketplace, the Vietnamese American author remain on the outside, positioned only to add details that endorse the American Dream and the American way of life.

As Nguyen slyly suggests, "Vietnamese Americans have the war, or perhaps the war has them,"[22] as *all* Vietnamese American authors are expected to anchor their work around a potentially divisive topic; if they do not, then their work is marked by the war's absence. No matter how inventive Vietnamese American literature becomes aesthetically, the readerly demand for the war fashions Vietnamese American writing into a volatile cultural product. Yet this particular form of attention can also be productive, as the demand to produce war stories gives Vietnamese American authors a forum in which to take on the contradictions created by the legacies of war and the associated geopolitical subterfuge. If, as Nguyen suggests, "the ghost that continues to tie Vietnam to America must be dealt with if Vietnamese American literature is to be more than ethnic literature that ultimately affirms America,"[23] then Vietnamese American authors can speak about pernicious global logics of capital, race, and governance to a ready-made audience who are eager to hear about the war. Instead of being read as just another entry in a run-on sentence of multicultural authors, Vietnamese American authors might use this interest in the war to direct readers to the complexity involved in the refugee experience in particular.

Perhaps this is why Nguyen bristles when *The Sympathizer* is described simply as an immigrant story rather than a refugee or war story. For Nguyen, the refugee story is an opportunity to tell the war story in a way that an American audience may neither want nor expect. As he succinctly expressed in a tweet from 22 April 2016, "To be an immigrant is to be part of the American Dream. To be a refugee is to be part of the American nightmare." When Vietnamese refugees are properly remembered as being part of the wartime experience, they can serve as a physical reminder of an embarrassing war that is continually recovered and papered over into victory through American-centric narratives. As Yến Lê Espiritu and Mimi Thi Nguyen have argued, the United States has tried to turn this lost war into a "good war" through the recuperation of the refugee figure—where the receiving state is positioned as a benevolent agent.[24] These narratives, of course, fail to acknowledge the geopolitical role that the United States played in creating Southeast Asian refugees to begin with. On the other hand, if refugees are written about in a way that expresses their own heterogeneity within the frame of a war narrative, then the unruly refugee body can leverage the interest in the war to open up space for a variety of social justice topics.

Writing as a refugee can be an act of refusal, upsetting the way that the Vietnam War is conventionally represented, placed, and considered within the confines of U.S. concerns. And due to the overwhelming abundance of American-centric narratives that exist both domestically and abroad, this "memory industry" can erase cultural and national histories that preceded U.S. intervention in Southeast Asia. In a National Public Radio interview, Nguyen explains that

> I'm a refugee and the story I'm telling is a war story because one of the ways that the United States tries to contain the meaning of these histories is to think that all of these Asians are here because they're immigrants, and that their story begins once they get to the United States. But again, my understanding is that many of these Asians are here because of the consequences of wars. And many immigrant stories and refugee stories need to be understood as war stories.[25]

In response, crafting and promoting a refugee story as a war story serves two purposes: first, it exposes the role that the United States has played in producing the conditions that create refugees, and second, it frames the movement and mobility of Vietnamese people in a manner that re-presents the past and makes the Vietnamese American present particularly germane for other immigrant and refugee populations.[26] Positioning *The Sympathizer* as a refugee story during interviews can be considered a pedagogical performance that provides context to the process of producing refugee subjects in an attempt to persuade the audience that refugee stories are a necessary continuation of, and counterpoint to, conventional war stories. For Nguyen, this is a process of countering accepted reading practices where "the refugee who becomes a writer is given the license to tell a refugee story, [but] he or she is not seen as writing an actual war story, at least not one that is given the same weight as a soldier's."[27]

In the interviews and promotional material that accompany *The Sympathizer,* there exists a rhetorical jostling between the attempts to locate and contextualize Nguyen and Nguyen's own positioning of himself. For instance, both high-profile reviews of his book in the *New York Times* claim that he is giving voice to the previously voiceless. Yet there is a stark difference between the groups of people whom the reviewers assume are "voiceless" and the people Nguyen represents in his book. To wit, the narrator in the novel is a North Vietnamese spy embedded in the upper echelons of the South Vietnamese Army, serving as a confidant of a South Vietnamese general he follows to the United States after the Fall of Saigon. Even through this narrator is a double agent who spends much of the book recording and recoding Vietnamese life of the North, the South, and indeed the Vietnamese American diaspora, Nguyen is presented in many reviews and interviews as providing a monolithic, previously voiceless "Vietnamese" side of the war. This ignores the many different sides of Vietnamese life that Nguyen offers up and the polyphonic, divergent voices that are produced in such an arrangement. Nguyen notes that the very idea of "the other side" or "the voiceless" is an Orientalizing binary gesture and that there is a fount of wartime writing by Vietnamese authors in Vietnam about the "second Indochina war" that comprise plenty of "voiced" Vietnamese accounts of the colonial war, if one takes the time to find them. The rhetorical imbalance, then, is not a matter of a need for a "Vietnamese account" but rather the effects of a powerful American memory industry that programmatically ignores the other accounts, or as Arundhati Roy's frames the quandary, "There's really no such thing as the 'voiceless.' There are only the deliberately silenced, or the preferably unheard."[28]

Nguyen is frequently called upon to be a translator or archaeologist who unearths the previously "lost" Vietnamese version of the war. But having a Vietnamese American stand in for the Vietnamese experience of the war, with little regard to the differences and history of Vietnamese people and Vietnamese Americans, silences Vietnamese American voices as well. Even though Nguyen is very forthright that he is a Vietnamese American whose family left Vietnam when he was four years old, his Vietnamese American voice remains unacknowledged and unheard when he is called to be Vietnam's voice. Nguyen's own publisher, Grove Press, traffics in the elision of Vietnamese American experiences to some extent when marketing Nguyen's book as the "new," "the fresh," and the "unheard." The press's breathless exaltation on its website sells the book as "a startling debut novel from a powerful new voice featuring one of the most remarkable narrators of recent fiction: a conflicted subversive idealist working as a double agent in the aftermath of the Vietnam War." Discerning whether or not *The Sympathizer* is one of the most remarkable narrators of recent fiction is a needless debate and perhaps risks taking promotional language too seriously, as who could make a claim about the entirety of recent fiction? But more tellingly, why should the reader be startled by Nguyen's book? By marketing the book as startling or surprising, Nguyen and his narrator are regarded as bringing something to the reader that is remarkably and perhaps radically different. Certainly, *The Sympathizer* is an innovative work written with a unique reflexive voice, but similar claims could be made about the books of other Vietnamese American refugee writers such as Vu Tran, Truong Tran, Linh Dinh, and many more. In other words, to those paying attention to the rich dialogue among authors, critics, and community members who create and promote Vietnamese American literature, another strong and accomplished Vietnamese American voice should not be much of a surprise. But to court a general reading public, these authors are perpetually delivered as "new," "different," and "other." Economies of the "never before heard of" position the Vietnamese American voice, once again, as foreign and outside the mainstream—even at a moment when, courtesy of the Pulitzer Prize, *The Sympathizer* has assumed center stage. However, Nguyen's genre choice could also be considered as a gesture that "secretly" confirms and subverts the book's own promotion. While the spy novel usually has a comfortable conventional arc that resolves the various conflicts in the interests of the state and/or status quo, Nguyen's refugee spy story elongates the temporality and geography of the war, weaving through various strata of social life to highlight the long-lasting affective and political consequences of wartime decisions.

The Refugee Spy Novel

Nguyen is certainly not the first Asian American to write this brand of genre fiction, with Ed Lin, Henry Chang, Don Lee, Naomi Hirahara, and, most famously, Chang Rae Lee all authoring spy, detective, or crime stories with Asian American themes, characters, and/or settings. Susan Koshy identifies the 1980s and 1990s in particular as a moment when the spy genre developed into a playful device used by Asian American authors. The spy story was a literary form that could be fashioned to frame the challenges Asian Americans faced as they were gaining a larger degree of societal recognition, where, as Koshy argues, "the passage from invisibility to recognition [was] a treacherous one . . . because recognition may again endorse racial difference however well intentioned."[29] During this period the spy genre became a way to creatively articulate the disconnect felt between racial expectations and subjective experience. More specifically, the tropes of spying, trespassing, and disguise could "reveal the gaps between the ideals of emancipation and equality that drove civil rights struggles and their outcome in the liberal pluralism of a multicultural polity where recognition of diversity reifies and congeals identities."[30] Tina Chen suggests that these acts of "impersonation" detail the complicated passage to recognition and describe the contortions required for individuals to embrace the multifarious category of Asian American itself. Serving as a textual and metatextual technique, impersonation "foreground[s] the limits of subjectivity" while also acknowledging the need to inhabit a subject position—suggesting that, in a spy story, impersonation should be read as an expression of Asian Americans' multiple allegiances rather than a trope that simply implies deceit or an embrace of the impostor position.[31] As the title of Chen's book *Double Agency* suggests, her reading of impersonation recognizes these multiple allegiances and sees impersonation as a way that Asian Americans claim agency to write their own selves into different forms of subjecthood.

Choosing to write *The Sympathizer* as a spy novel provides Nguyen with the generic versatility necessary to craft a narrator unique to Vietnamese American fiction while also presenting the reader with a dangerous figure who transgresses conventional representations of the refugee. A biracial loner who gains credibility throughout the book with his ability to see multiple sides of a situation, the narrator displays an ethical and ethnic elusiveness that troubles the impulses of an audience who may be eager to consume the Vietnamese and/or Vietnamese American experience as a stable entity. Adding to this tactical obfuscation is that the narrator's hardened voice, stylistically, is removed enough to create a universalist allure and also provides the reader with intimate, subjective details that would normally only be familiar to a cultural insider. Most cultural-insider texts with commercial ambition encounter the problem of having to translate ethnicity for their audience or being marketed toward a niche readership who has already decided the culture is worth consuming. The spy novel, on the other hand, is a popular genre that courts a broad swath of readers who likely fall outside the audience of those usually attracted to tales of the American immigrant experience. To this new group of readers, the book promises international intrigue and presents them with existential quandaries of right and wrong, loyalty and progress, and attention to self and other. At first blush these problematics seem like universal quandaries, yet in their contextual application Nguyen can rewrite history to demonstrate how the refugee experience profoundly shapes and troubles both state and ethical borders.

The spy novel as refugee story troubles the easy nod to sympathy that usually accompanies tales of downtrodden refugee life and redemption. As Nguyen himself contends, "The idea that refugees are victims simply becomes a way of not sympathizing with them. We continue to treat them as less than humans. If you see people only as victims and therefore as less than human, they're still not the same as you are."[32] Indeed, essential to Nguyen's scholarly criticism is the idea that one must see the inhuman, or potential for inhumanity, in the self and "the other" before both can be fully appreciated as active human agents.[33] Narratively in *The Sympathizer,* this inhumanity is found in characters who gain power through nefarious means, speak out of turn, and behave in ways that run counter to notions of gender and racial equality. Nearly everyone in the story is flawed and willing to shift alliances at a moment's notice, and the narrator himself is involved in rapes and killings including one that involves "a relatively innocent man, which is the best one could hope for in this world."[34] While the figure of an antihero is not new to American accounts of the Vietnam War, the antihero familiar to American readers is a white American soldier or veteran disillusioned with the ethical and moral quagmires that develop during wartime. This presents the white American as a complex and divided figure who stands, allegorically, for the U.S. nation, while Vietnamese people and interests remain singular and muted. As the war is fought abroad—over there—the return of the veteran back home allows for a clean separation between here and there and provides a convenient endpoint to the war's conclusion. However, by presenting an untrustworthy transnational spy as the protagonist, Nguyen's biracial Vietnamese antihero troubles the clear divide between Vietnamese and American interests, and having him involved in the Vietnamese American refugee community extends the time frame of the war's afterlife. The narrator's multiple allegiances suggest that he cannot easily be read as an allegory for any particular nation, and presenting numerous Vietnamese American figures who have rational yet fluid moral sensibilities runs counter to the usual presentations of refugees as powerless masses.

The narrator, while subject to many political and personal agendas, remains composed throughout most of the book, cutting a suave, cunning, and at times swaggering figure. He is not a powerless refugee but rather an agent who reveals that everyone—North Vietnamese, South Vietnamese, refugees, the United States—is culpable and part of this global drama. Nguyen's attraction to spy novels was in part because they

> typically operate as first-person narratives for formal reasons—you're embedded in this person's point of view, creating an unreliable narration. But that also allows a great degree of intimacy with this person's voice. . . . I

wanted the narration to be extremely intimate, and that you would be carried along with his emotions and his ideas.... I liked the fact that I'd be forcing the reader to empathize with this person. Someone who's probably quite alien to most people and does things that most would consider to be objectionable or reprehensible.[35]

This swaggering "bad refugee" upsets many of the pernicious model-minority stereotypes often attributed to Asian Americans and in their place provides a complex and ambiguous vision of Vietnameseness written on Nguyen's own terms. The intimacy of the spy's first-person narration forces the reader to not only observe but also empathize with an unusual character, and in this account the readers are presented with waves of emotions and ideas rather than something akin to a stable psychological portrait. Nguyen's spy protagonist thus serves as a central node that provides Nguyen with the versatility to travel through various social types, class positions, and notions that were circulating around the refugee community during this period. Again, his scholarly research is evident in this move, as Nguyen is forthright that he modeled many of the characters and moments in the book after actual people and events, using extensive archival material to mold this fictional yet plausible world.

David Seed offers that the spy novel differs from the detective story insofar as there is no discreet crime involved; rather, there is a "covert action that ... transgresses conventional, moral, or legal boundaries."[36] Further, undercover agents are actively involved in the world of deception, marking their own actions as similar to those lurking in the realms they investigate. The figure of the insider/outsider spy gives Nguyen the flexibility to create a deceptive "ethnic" character who does not belong to any social group—a literal bastard outside of familial lineage and communal alliance.[37] Throughout the book the narrator takes great pride in being set apart from the masses, and when he does seemingly take a side, the group serves as a cover for his eventual subterfuge. The narrator meets his communist coconspirator, Man, in Catholic churches, reveling to the pleasures of hiding among the believers in plain view, disguising himself as devout while in fact reveling in the blasphemy and the transgressions. In contrast to spy novelist John Le Carré's characters who strike out against soulless bureaucracy, Nguyen's narrator is most critical of those who too easily or stably identify with their station in life, whether this encompasses their military affiliation, ethnic position, or national allegiance. In this context the individualism of Nguyen's narrator is determined by the contexts surrounding his birth, and while the narrator is sympathetic, he is equally unrelenting in his assessment of others around him. Nguyen's world is one where firm alliances are few, self-interest is rampant, and just actions go unrewarded. Yet even though it is gritty and cynical, this world is not altogether bleak. The narrator's ability to see both sides of a scenario allows him to carefully navigate the wide variety of scenes and social settings that he finds himself in. Weaving through these different social groups provides a bountiful source of readerly pleasure, and the narrator's wry remarks about the people he meets build a conspiratorial intimacy that indeed foists culpability onto the reader, who chuckles along. The majority of the book is written as a confession to his captor, and the intimate address the narrator uses gradually pulls the audience into the position of a trusted friend or at times an accomplice. The narrator shares with readers the details that, as a double agent, he cannot say aloud, assuring the reader that despite his dashing exterior, he really is in many ways like "us"—a bond shared between the nameless narrator and the nameless reader.

Yet this complicit comradeship ultimately exposes the ethically dubious proposition that either the narrator or the reader can think of themselves as sympathizers who unproblematically see the other side. As David Palumbo-Liu argues in *The Deliverance of Others: Reading in a Global Age* (2012), contemporary global novels are valued in the literary marketplace by how much otherness they can deliver to the consuming public. Of course, in this exercise, readers regulate and choose the amount of otherness that they want to take in; therefore, at the level of the literary marketplace there is a constant calibration and recalibration of what kinds of otherness is acceptable. Nguyen's decision to write in the spy novel genre was in part a way to highlight this act of discerning and placing otherness. Central to this enterprise is the malleable moral compass of his protagonist and the seemingly measured way that he accesses the world around him. Nguyen speaks at length about not knowing what this fictional work was going to be about until he found the voice of the narrator, and in interviews he repeatedly identifies the opening lines of the book as defining the tone and themes that would unfold throughout the rest of the book. These lines begin with "I am a spy, a sleeper, a spook, a man of two faces. Perhaps not surprisingly, I am also a man of two minds. I am not some misunderstood mutant from a comic book or a horror movie, although some have treated me as such. I am simply able to see any issue from both sides."[38] In this opening, explicitly crafted to be memorable, the narrator describes this ability to see both sides as a "talent," which suggests that he has an extraordinary ability to process multiple points of view as well as an expertise in mediating the flow of otherness. Having this guide that can access Vietnamese, American, and Vietnamese American communities lures readers into thinking that they will receive the balanced account of the Vietnam War missing from previous iterations of the war story. However, Nguyen slowly subverts this reading through his unreliable narrator, and when the narrator finds himself being tortured close to the conclusion of the book, it becomes clear that there are certain events he has left out of his previous account to the commandant and the reader. What is revealed in this moment is that his ability to see any issue from both sides falls short—as he has not been able or willing to live each issue from all sides at once—and cannot trust himself to remember and represent others in a manner that gives voice to the plurality of actors he encounters. This revelation fundamentally brings into question the very means of knowledge production the reader is participating in while exposing the narrator's and the reader's desire to think of themselves as unproblematically seeing the other side.

Exploring the ability and limits of seeing multiple sides was a central theme in the first Asian American spy novel with grand literary ambition, Chang-Rae Lee's *Native Speaker*. In Lee's book, which mixes the genre's fascination with clandestine operations and includes an extensive commentary on American race relations, "the spy's 'multiple roles,'" states Tina Chen, "are a logical extension of his personal history as a Korean American struggling to negotiate the divide that separates how others perceive him and how he sees himself."[39] As opposed to a detective novel where the reader follows along with the protagonist (and his or her perspective) to solve a central crime, both Nguyen's and Lee's novels play with what Chen calls "the trope of undetectability"—when protagonists are dropped into a multiplicity of spaces where they are able to pass as native.[40] Indeed, both Asian American protagonists find that the ability to move fluidly through spaces is a thrilling act, as conventionally they are told to stay "in their place." That is not to suggest that either protagonist is beyond race; on the contrary, their racial features and ethnic knowledge provide them with distinct tools that separate them from other investigators. In both cases the protagonists are not trying to be James Bond, the ultimate cosmopolitan. Rather, their profoundly local racialized performances mark them as unique, valued, and seemingly irreplaceable agents for both the organizations they serve and the reader.

Of course, framing *The Sympathizer* as a refugee spy novel distinguishes Nguyen's work from Lee's. Tina Chen suggests that Lee's work does not attempt to speak for social and political programs and instead deconstructs the genre itself to upset conventional forms of reading and stereotyping. Nguyen's work, on the other hand, wears its political and literary ambitions more openly and directly. Whereas with the Asian American spy novel, as outlined by Chen, spying becomes more than a metaphor for the "cultural dilemmas" faced by Asian Americans, where "the genre of the spy story affects the ways . . . acts of (self)-impersonation can be narrated and understood," Nguyen's refugee spy story involves the above (as an Asian American story itself) but also illuminates the contortions necessary for refugees to speak when read through a backdrop of American war. In the Asian American spy story, the tension hinges on how a minority subject position and ethnicity can be enunciated in a U.S. context; however, in addition the Vietnamese American refugee spy story requires the protagonist to reckon with how a homeland can be achieved.

In the book and in his promotion of *The Sympathizer,* Nguyen seeks no less than to rewrite the history of the Vietnam War and its aftermath in America. Reluctant to have readers approach *The Sympathizer* as a character study, Nguyen openly calls out American ignorance regarding the Vietnam War and in an interview with Tavis Smiley on national television stated "that most Americans knew nothing of what had happened to the Vietnamese people. They understood what happened to Americans, but for the Vietnamese and other Southeast Asians, a complete blank."[41] Again, instead of being satisfied with generic literary play, Nguyen doubles down on his professorial credentials to do this work of filling in the blanks by redirecting conversation.

Specifically, Nguyen steers conversation toward his own place within the scholarship and activism that define the history and present of Asian American studies. Nowhere was this more evident than in his public Facebook post following his Pulitzer Prize win:

> We all owe so much to the collective struggles and activists that preceded us, that laid the foundations for our individual achievement, to everyone lucky enough to be remembered and so many who have been forgotten. Great love to Asian American Studies, to Ethnic Studies, to UC Berkeley, my alma mater that made me into the person that I am, to all who fight the good fight and who will never, ever believe that they are only individuals.

So, while Nguyen's struggle with the book was, in his own words, "learning not to write like an academic," we should not be blind to the notion that this refugee novel overflows with academic concerns in its genesis, marketing, and literary execution. Indeed, the final sixth of the novel, where the narrator undergoes excruciating torture at the hands of the commandant, is deliberately written in a difficult and disorienting manner—undoing the intimacy, comfort, and trust built throughout the previous three hundred pages while deviating from the genre's conventions of leaving the reader with a comfortable orderly world. Even though *The Sympathizer* presents many of the broad themes, settings, and characters common to the spy genre, this is not a novel written for mass consumption. While Nguyen has certainly reached audiences larger than most other Asian American literary writers, he was not writing by the word, and the book does not have the action, dialogue, and narrative pacing common to dime-store spy novels. Rather, it is filled with literary allusions, is thoroughly researched, and attempts to tell the story in a way that can be interpreted on multiple levels at once. Nguyen's incursion into the genre anticipates the desire to reify and congeal different identities, and in response he presents readers with an elusive protagonist who is difficult to place, a narrator who embraces a multiplicity of roles and positions that trouble recognizable identity categories. While these uncertainties may discomfort the conventional reader of the spy novel, I argue that through his promotional enterprises Nguyen offers himself—the author and refugee—as a trustworthy remedy to these interpretive quandaries, framing himself as a palatable (yet secretly calculating) guide.

Conclusion: Clandestinity and the Refugee

Immigrants are used to being invisible in everyday life, only to be put under intense scrutiny during times of crisis.[42] Thus, it is no coincidence that the opening paragraph of *The Sympathizer* is inspired by and echoes Ralph Ellison's *The Invisible Man,* a book where racialized minorities remain invisible until they are acknowledged as threatening. Speaking about this lineage in an interview with Kerri Miller, Nguyen suggests that "Vietnamese people were [also] invisible until they became a threat . . . during the Vietnam War . . . so [the challenge became] how could I write a novel that responded to that crisis from the perspective of the invisible person?"[43] Positioning his book next to Ellison's classic places *The Sympathizer* within a literary tradition of ethnic American fiction that identifies and critiques the sociopolitical contexts, aesthetics, and institutions that determine how racial others are seen—or oftentimes not seen. And indeed, in response both books are alike insofar as they embrace the "threat" that these invisible actors can pose to others and to themselves.

As a clandestine spy, *The Sympathizer's* narrator embodies this invisible ethnic threat, with danger lurking behind his placid surface. And similarly, I have been demonstrating that Nguyen hides the countercultural qualities of his own position as an ethnic studies professor under the coifed and charming persona of the literary celebrity. As *The Sympathizer* was strategically released on 30 April 2015, exactly forty years after the Fall of Saigon, every aspect of how the book was promoted wears the war's history on its sleeve. But in calling attention to the linkages between the war and its aftermath, Nguyen writes a work of refugee literature that, in the words of Marguerite Nguyen and Catherine Fung, combines "refugee ethics that elicit the care of the international community . . . with . . . refugee aesthetics, which reveal how the complex histories, geopolitics, and memories of refugee migrations are . . . brought into view in ways that might not be apparent in what is explicitly said."[44] In this light, Viet Thanh Nguyen's incursion into refugee aesthetics demands that his audience think comparatively across different acts of storytelling, war, and memory making while modeling the practical and ethical challenges of attempting to do so through his narrator "of two minds."[45] Nguyen helps the audience along on both a performative and an aesthetic level by demonstrating to his readers that refugees still exist, shaping the fabric of the United States even as many attempt to forget their presence and/or the events that brought them to America. Indeed, the act of writing *The Sympathizer* is a reminder that the ways this seemingly invisible population is received and remembered can still be altered through aesthetic force and the strategic mediation of reading practices.

Through his work Nguyen informs his audience that the ethics involved in eliciting care for the refugee is different from eliciting pity, and for Nguyen embracing the full political potential of the refugee position requires speaking up and speaking out about sensitive topics that can upset both the readership and the represented community. As he relates, "Many Vietnamese refugees feel the Americans betrayed by [the United States] pulling out, but they would never say it publicly in English . . . because the Vietnamese people are grateful to America for rescuing them, and they don't want to contaminate that narrative. But I'm willing to because it's what is said in private, and Americans need to hear this complexity."[46] While "contaminating" common narratives could be a risky move, readers inundated Nguyen with letters after the release of *The Sympathizer*, eagerly confessing that they never knew that the events described in the novel had happened to Vietnamese people—even when these letter writers resided in places such as Westminster, California, a city where thousands of Vietnamese refugees and their descendants live.[47] Reading this spy novel, these readers were drawn into an intimate relationship with the protagonist, intrigued by his emotions, ideas, and points of view, rather than being consumed with the search for an ethnic social type. The publishing industry, however, can hinder ethnic American authors' ability to reach these broader audiences: despite its genre-bending premise, Chang-Rae Lee's *Native Speaker* was marketed by its own publisher only as an "immigrant novel" rather than a "spy thriller."[48] This rigidity in the conventional promotional structures of mainstream publishing industries suggests that leaving the reception of a book to the whims of the market is too risky for an Asian American author with lasting literary ambition, which explains the importance of Nguyen's decision to aggressively educate and speak out to readers when marketing his own book.

In his media appearances, Viet Thanh Nguyen presents a public figure who thrives as a refugee rooted in the United States and indeed expresses a complex patriotism that the first generation of Vietnamese Americans simply did not have the representational opportunities to perform or achieve. And Nguyen has created the imaginative ground that allows him to perform as a refugee subject who can call the United States home, both securely and critically, through his complex aestheticization of the refugee predicament, present in *The Sympathizer*. The ability to understand the relationship between individual acts and collective action is a talent common to both the spy and the public intellectual, and Nguyen sees himself "as a writer who's writing his books alone in his room, but who also imagines himself, in collaboration, in solidarity, with many other political and social movements outside of literature."[49] One could say, then, that as an author Nguyen serves as a backroom agent for these political and social movements while leveraging his literary celebrity, personality, and pedagogical talent to maneuver his book into the American literary canon. As he succeeds in garnering market and literary success, his work becomes a vehicle to circulate ideas generated by ethnic American social and political movements among multiple generations and audiences. Traversing the gaps that exist between academia, publishers, and the greater reading public, Nguyen has successfully created a book peppered with the generic pleasures of a spy novel while also feeding the American reader's desire for war stories—but via a complicated refugee voice. Instead of being satisfied with momentary market success, he has spoken out through his interviews and his refugee story about race, power, and representation in the hope that a refugee personality can have a lasting and perhaps even permanent impact on the literary and social imagination of the United States.

Refugee Futures

A Conclusion

Displacing a singular refugee aesthetic with the complexity of refugee aesthetics is anything but simple, for disrupting an aesthetic regime requires remediating both the production and consumption of images that figure refugees as distant, needy, and perpetually transient. To combat the rigid patterns common to the preexisting refugee image, a group of Southeast Asian American authors have assumed the refugee position whereby refugees use aesthetic force to redefine how their work and experiences are received. The Southeast Asian American refugee population has had to negotiate an intense convergence of television, photographic, and newspaper coverage but are now, in turn, leveraging this media-soaked position to comment on the social inequalities that produce and persist in refugee life while transforming the perniciously stable and historically flattened refugee figure into an agent of social change. Nowhere is this more apparent than in the work of Viet Thanh Nguyen, who in his novels and short stories refashions the broad category of refugee humanity into refugee personalities that are variably flawed, strong, irrational, and wise—showing how the reification of refugee life neglects the complexities of everyday experience and can diminish the literary value and aesthetic force of refugee writing. Instead of relying on others to circumscribe their place in the world, refugee artists and authors have taken an active role in remapping their pasts and presents, imaginatively identifying roles and spaces where refugees can live, grow, and even flourish in the future.

Yet to talk about refugee futures requires thinking about refuge in an unconventional way. As refuge is designed to be a temporary and exceptional status, the future of refugees is ideally that they will disappear; although, as the number of refugees around the world continues to grow, it is clear that refugees are here to stay, and accordingly, so are the creative and psychic forces of refugee life. The future poses two potential crises for Southeast Asian American refugee aesthetic production, however. First, as the Southeast Asian American population ages and as incoming migrants no longer qualify for legal refugee status, refuge is becoming an event that occurred increasingly further in the past. To tell the complex story of refugee life, refuge might be best theorized and written about by newer refugee groups facing different technologies, social structures, and political systems. Second, a more reflexive and detailed style of refugee story is now being recognized and codified, with a number of authors who are not refugees themselves creating refugee stories that follow familiar patterns and beats, leaving the place and importance of actual refugee artists unclear.

At the moment, refugee authors are at the vanguard of a refugee literary style that includes an exposition of multiple subject positions, a concern with interior life, and a critical reflexivity regarding the material forces that encourage the production of refugee narratives. However, the relative success of these authors in the literary and artistic marketplace has inspired nonrefugee authors to produce refugee stories that are similarly more nuanced than traditional humanizing narratives. An example of a nonrefugee author engaging this newly codified refugee style can be found in Canadian writer Lawrence Hill's novel *The Illegal* (2015), which details the life of Kieta Ali, a long-distance runner who leaves "Zontoroland" after his dissident journalist father is killed by the government. Following the complications involved in Ali seeking refuge in "Freedom State,"

Hill writes in the first-person perspective of numerous Freedom State characters, creating an intricate map of the different government officials, protestors, and special interests who become involved in refugee life. A comfortable book for middlebrow readers, *The Illegal* offers a happy ending where a disparate group of plucky individuals successfully pull together to help Ali ultimately achieve citizenship. Despite the book's easy conclusion, intricately mapping the numerous people and structures involved in sustaining refugee life implicitly asks audiences to locate themselves among the various agential forces in the story. Indeed, Hill states that one of the reasons why he staged this drama in an imaginary space is that "it's easier for the reader to step into it without feeling personally challenged,"[1] luring an audience not necessarily invested in refugee life into thinking about the patterns and customs created by refuge. Using this imaginary space allows Hill to compile some of the most egregious governmental policies created around the world, demonstrate their inefficiency, and model for the reader successful social responses to these policies.

Ali's refugee plight is staged mostly in the two imagined countries of Zontoroland and Freedom State, but minor characters and events from existing nation-states such as France, Ethiopia, and Canada are also included. Much like in Mohsin Hamid's *Exit West*, this artful geographic plotting of unnamed or imaginary places alongside actual nation-states subtly directs the attention of the reader outside of the fictive world, identifying the creation and maintenance of refugee life as a circuit that functions across different countries on multiple legislative, material, and rhetorical levels. Distilling the patterns of governmental rhetoric, policy, and enforcement that put these people on the move, Hill identifies the events and procedures that fashion refugee life. Using the form of near-dystopian fiction to aestheticize the formal continuities of these procedures brings to light how various interests and kinds of rhetoric seemingly follow refugees endlessly, turning the novel into a tool that illuminates what is in effect a refugee script. While certainly valuable on a macrolevel, what is limiting about this scripting of the refugee experience into middlebrow writing is that unlike in

Viet Thanh Nguyen's *The Sympathizer*, the comfortable ending lets the reader off the hook, turning refugee literature from a socially urgent force into a palatable form of genre fiction. This refugee-genre fiction enables those outside of the refugee community to briefly contemplate refugee lives but cast the book aside once the narrative ends, as the characters and government agencies of Zontoroland and Freedom State do not really exist outside of the text itself, nor is the author intimately rooted or necessarily implicated in the shaping of refugee life.[2]

Prominent visual artist Ai Weiwei is another nonrefugee figure interested in drawing attention to the refugee experience, engaging with refugee aesthetics through grand installations that span both museum and in public spaces.[3] Leveraging a method that Thomas O. Haakenson identifies as "present absence," Weiwei employs a "strategy of utilizing victims' absent bodies" to focus on "regional or even global policies around refugees, migration, and access."[4] Producing a stunning public installation that called attention to the refugees fleeing Syria and other Middle Eastern countries, in 2016 Weiwei wrapped fourteen thousand used life jackets that had washed up on the beach of the Greek island of Lesbos around the columns of Berlin's Konzerthaus, alluding to those who died during refuge or are otherwise absent from conventional representational forms. Another example of his grand renderings of the refugee experience is his 2017 museum installation *Law of the Journey*, consisting of massive replicas of lifeboats filled with crowded masses of faceless identical refugee figures, some of whom had spilled out of the boats and lay, presumably dead, on the museum floor.

While Weiwei's interventions into refugee aesthetics are undoubtedly moving and stunning, particularly due to their experiments with scale and the creative ways that he includes those who are usually absent, these spectacles ultimately bring attention to the refugee crisis through typical appeals to humanity at large rather than nuancing of refugee life itself. Weiwei's own framing underlines this compulsion to universalize. In the exhibition material of the *Law of the Journey* he states, "There is no refugee crisis . . . [,] there is only a human crisis. In dealing with refugees we've lost our basic human values."[5]

And in a 2018 piece in *The Guardian* he opines, "The refugee crisis isn't about refugees. It's about us."[6] Even on an aesthetic level, Weiwei's widely distributed documentary *Human Flow* is dominated by shots of water, boats, masses of bodies, infinity lines, and camps, relying on conventional refugee archetypes to draw in audiences while providing few unfamiliar comments about the refugees or the kinds of attention they receive. So, even though he extends the reach of the refugee story to different audiences and draws a great amount of attention to the hardships that refugees endure in innovative ways, in the end his formal interventions do not significantly move beyond the interpretive framework of the conventional refugee aesthetic formula, further reinforcing stereotypes about refugees and the centrality of the viewer.

Considering the amount of public attention that nonrefugee artists and authors such as Hill, Hamid, and Weiwei garner through their imaginative takes on refugee stories and exhibitions, where does this leave actual refugees and refugee artists? Are refugee artists, once again, stuck with the familiar burden of authenticity as the most potent form of expression? And then will this lead back to texts that must further excavate memories and details of hardship? One way that refugee authors Monique Truong and Viet Thanh Nguyen combat these conservative stylistic retreats is to instead mislead their audiences through untrustworthy narrators.[7] Since what constitutes an authentic refugee and Vietnamese American voice has been overdetermined during the past forty years, presenting information, voices, and personas through untrustworthy narrators confuses and indeed comments upon what is expected from refugee voices. In this light, creating an unreliable narrator undermines and contradicts the very foundations of what is demanded of refugee voices, for refugee voices are often sought out to present "the other side of the story," which is expected to provide a particular type of "truth" that will help buttress various kinds of rescue narratives.

For example, *The Sympathizer* goes well beyond giving voice to the previously voiceless, spurring the reader to read more suspiciously by presenting a charming yet untrustworthy lead character with rakish charm and fatal flaws. Presenting as a "bad refugee," Nguyen's protagonist seems at first to be a less than sympathetic character who revels, somewhat selfishly, in his border crossing and code switching. However, as he comes to feel the pull of conflicting geopolitical interests, Nguyen's refugee protagonist is left to construct alliances across numerous social classes, nations, and political causes. And as the story unravels he attempts to figure out, as a solitary agent, his own role in this global drama. In this light it seems that he is not necessarily a "bad" person; rather, he is a flawed antihero who needs time to figure out his place in this world and will figure it out in the end. Or so we think. Near the conclusion of the book we learn that the narrator has misrepresented the rape of an affiliated secret agent, in the process hiding from the reader his own complicity in the event. Although we might understand that he is not so much lying to the reader as lying to himself, his inability to speak the truth comments on the difficulties that a refugee may have when required to tell an entire "side of the story."

For young Cambodian American writers similarly burdened by the demand for authenticity, the complex and reflexive voice offered by refugee aesthetics has been useful in creating alternatives to the "trauma narratives" that dominate and loom over the literary reception of diasporic Cambodian literature. As Cambodian American writer Monika Sok relates, "Like many Cambodian Americans of the 1.5 and second generation, I read survival literature to piece together my history.... But sometimes I worry that the world reduces Cambodians, tokenizing my people inside a trauma narrative."[8] A robust refugee position that expresses the pressures of having to represent the other side offers strategies for these writers to resist and negotiate with "a white publishing industry that eats up trauma."[9] Writing refugee *fiction* in particular can provide the flexibility to break away from these expectations by using the details of the Cambodian refugee experience to reenvision key moments in U.S. domestic history. For instance, Angela So relates that she turned to fiction to write a "kind of dystopian speculative novel about the second Dust Bowl ... [,] which is like writing about what it means to be a refugee, and so for me the dust storm lets me imagine what it means to be a refugee in your own country."[10] For Cambodian American poet Sokunthary Svay, creative approaches give Cambodian American writers the chance to be entertaining and humorous, adding that it "occurred to me that I can put anything on the page that I want. And that's a *huge* revelation for me."[11] And while she includes the voices and experiences of her mother in her poems, her work foregrounds Svay's own experiences with her mother instead of trafficking in her mother's monadic authenticity. This gives Svay the elasticity to highlight moments of what Cathy Schlund-Vials calls "refugee unfamiliarity"[12] that counter the notion that Cambodian Americans are effortlessly bicultural and authentic figures. Instead, ethnic disarticulation is on display—exemplified in Svay's poetry through her ambivalent experiences with the Khmer language and the cultural dislocation that she feels during her return visit to Cambodia.

This approach recognizes that experience necessarily has its own limits, and demanding a truthful and authentic retelling of refugee experiences creates its own set of aesthetic distortions. Consequently, locating the place of refugees and refugee production in the global imagination requires understanding that when a refugee experience is communicated it becomes an aesthetic product that, to paraphrase Stuart Hall, is a floating signifier that carries its own set of relational meanings that are shaped by, but not fully representative of and contained by, the myriad of realities that refugees face.[13] While de-linking refugee experience from refugee aesthetics is important, as it allows refugee artistic work to be read as something other than ontology, it does leave the category disturbingly open. For if the aesthetic is indeed limitless, then there is nothing in particular that refugee aesthetics offers other than a set of tropes or styles.

Perhaps, though, there is evidence that the refugee experience can forge a critical consciousness that not only describes what happened during refuge but also has an acute sense of what is to be done.[14] While nonrefugee artists are dipping their toes into refugee aesthetics, Southeast Asian American artists and organizations have taken the lead in creating spaces that nurture refugee dialogues, cultivating a vanguard of refugee expression. For instance, an organization such as the Diasporic Vietnamese

American Artist Network creates forums, talks, and writing retreats that allow Southeast Asian diasporic artists to stay at the forefront of refugee thought through intergenerational, transnational, and cross-ethnic artistic dialogue.[15] In addition, the acquisition and curating of collections at the Orange County Southeast Asian American archive at the University of California–Irvine, the grants and programming provided by the Critical Refugee Studies Collective,[16] the Triennial Southeast Asian American Studies conference, and a growing network of committed scholars of the Southeast Asian American experience help refugee art, literature, and politics move from a marginal Asian American interest to a central contributor to the discipline of Asian American studies. Further, these organizations help refugee stories and art become something that connects Southeast Asian American experience to other ethnic American and international voices and interests.

Developing in tandem with these organizations is the emergence of the refugee consumer. No longer are refugee authors solely reliant on audiences outside of their communities to consume their work, as Southeast Asian Americans and other refugee groups are gaining footholds in economic, social, and academic arenas. While it may not be economically sustainable to market only to these communities, these audiences can provide the bump needed for successful writers and artists to sustain their work on their own terms. The academic study and promotion of Asian American work should not be discounted as a market force either, as the dissemination, promotion, and scholarship about refugee work helps to position this art so it can be iconoclastic and taste making rather than having to cater to the existing tastes of others. And again, agencies such as the Smithsonian Asian Pacific American Center and the Asian American Literary Review provide infrastructure, promotional materials, and events that can build and reach diverse audiences. These institutions become meeting places where refugees can continue to generate awareness and ideas about the intertwined relationship between aesthetics and market tactics, for promoting refugee aesthetics involves jostling across the different community organizations, political agencies, and media forms that ultimately choose where, when, and how refugee images are disseminated.

With these ongoing battles over market selection and the ways that narratives are received, it is important to distinguish the project of refugee aesthetics from the category of Southeast Asian American writing or art, for the refugee position is a choice and a strategy. Understanding of the power and circulation of refugee aesthetics makes possible new patterns of speaking up and speaking out that knowledgeably assess and track the outcomes of global capital, domestic policy, and colonial logic. This can include the voices of those who, as a group, have not yet gained the legal designation and privileges of being a refugee, and refugee aesthetics can provide a space and style to advocate for their inclusion through more equitable and just refugee policies. In this light, battles over refugee aesthetics are not a matter of trying to reclaim past experiences but instead are attempts to claim *the ability* to tell stories of refugee life. This means that these stories do not belong to the refugees themselves, but their continual existence provides an opportunity for refugees and others to reimagine how refuge, refugee art, and refugee life should exist in the future.

Notes

Introduction

1. Sophie Gilbert, "*Exit West* and the Edge of Dystopia," book review of *Exit West* by Mohsin Hamid, *The Atlantic*, 8 Mar 2017.

2. For further discussion of "the refugee condition," see Mimi Thi Nguyen, *The Gift of Freedom: War, Debt, and Other Refugee Passages* (Durham, NC: Duke University Press, 2012), 53.

3. Liisa Malkki, "Speechless Emissaries: Refugees, Humanitarianism, and Dehistoricization," *Cultural Anthropology* 11.3 (1996): 389.

4. Chris George, "Opening of 'Unpacked Refugee Baggage'—Panel," Artspace, New Haven, CT, 15 October 2017.

5. Indeed, Southeast Asian Americans were not even the first Asian American refugee population. As Madeline Y. Hsu explains, "approximately 32,000 Chinese . . . gained entry or permanent residency in the United States through refugee legislation and procedures between 1948 and 1966" (12). That this highly educated group of refugees has been more or less forgotten, according to Hsu, reinforces my point regarding how dominant the Southeast Asian example has been in defining the aesthetic qualities of refugees in the American imagination. See Madeline Y. Hsu, "The Disappearance of America's Cold War Chinese Refugees, 1948–1966," *Journal of American Ethnic History* 31.4 (2012): 12–33.

6. Fiona Ngô, Mimi Thi Nguyen, and Mariam B. Lam, "Southeast Asian American Studies Special Issue: Guest Editors' Introduction," *Positions: East Asia Cultures Critique* 20.3 (2012): 671.

7. Ibid., 672.
8. Ibid., 673.
9. Ibid.
10. Cathy J. Schlund-Vials, "The Subjects of 1975: Delineating the Necessity of Critical Refugee Studies," *MELUS: Multi-Ethnic Literature of the U.S.* 41.3 (2016): 200.
11. While there have certainly been many important "critical" studies of refugees (Hannah Arendt, Giorgio Agamben, Liisa Malkki, etc.), Yến Lê Espiritu has coined critical refugee studies as "an interdisciplinary field that re-conceptualized the refugee not as an object of rescue, but as a site of social and political critiques, whose emergence when traced, made visible the processes of colonization, war, and displacement." This emerging field is developing through the University of California's Critical Refugee Studies Collective, and the above definition is taken from its organizing statement "Towards Critical Refugee Studies: Being and Becoming in Exceptional States of War, Violence, and Militarism," available at https://uchri.org/awards/toward-critical-refugee-studies-being-and-becoming-in-exceptional-states-of-war-violence-and-militarism/.
12. Embracing the refugee position in this way also challenges what Paul Gilroy describes as "the continuing aspiration to acquire [an identity that is] supposedly authentic, natural, and stable." See Paul Gilroy, "The Black Atlantic as a Counterculture of Modernity," *Theorizing Diaspora: A Reader*, ed. Jana Evans Blackwell and Anita Mannur (New York: Blackwell, 2003), 67.
13. Terry Eagleton, *The Ideology of the Aesthetic* (New York: Blackwell, 1991).
14. Bill Ashcroft, "Towards a Postcolonial Aesthetics," *Journal of Postcolonial Writing* 51.4 (2015): 410.
15. The full text of Article 1(A)(2) of the 1951 convention is as follows: "As a result of events occurring before 1 January 1951 and owing to a well-founded fear of being persecuted for reasons of race, religion, nationality, membership of a particular social group or political opinion, is outside the country of his nationality and is unable, or owing to such fear, is unwilling to avail himself of the protection of that country; or who, not having a nationality and being outside the country of his former habitual residence as a result of such events, is unable or, owing to such fear, is unwilling to return to it." The 1967 "Protocol Relating to the Status of Refugees" removed the temporal determinants (of 1951) and also expanded the geographic scope of the article, as previously it was understood to refer only to events occurring in Europe.
16. April Shemak, *Asylum Speakers: Caribbean Refugees and Testimonial Discourse* (New York: American Literatures Initiative, 2010), 3.
17. Christopher Lee, *The Semblance of Identity: Aesthetic Mediation in Asian American Literature* (Stanford, CA: Stanford University Press, 2012), 16.

18. Kandice Chuh, *The Difference Aesthetics Makes: On the Humanities "after Man"* (Durham, NC: Duke University Press, 2019), xii.

19. See Edward Said, *Culture and Imperialism* (New York: Knopf, 1993), xiii, 20.

20. Mikhail Bakhtin, *Art and Answerability: Early Philosophical Essays by M. M. Bakhtin,* ed. Michael Holquist and Vladimir Liapunov. (Austin: University of Texas Press, 1990), 264.

21. Min Hyoung Song, *The Children of 1965: On Writing, and Not Writing, as an Asian American* (Durham, NC: Duke University Press, 2013), 3.

22. Mimi Thi Nguyen, *The Gift of Freedom: War, Debt, and Other Refugee Passages* (Durham, NC: Duke University Press, 2012), 5.

23. Chuh, *The Difference Aesthetics Makes,* 16.

24. Liisa Malkki, "Speechless Emissaries: Refugees, Humanitarianism, and Dehistoricization," *Cultural Anthropology* 11.3 (1996): 384.

25. Phuong Tran Nguyen, *Becoming Refugee American: The Politics of Rescue in Little Saigon* (Champaign: University of Illinois Press, 2017), 2.

26. Christine Buckley, "'Good Refugees' and 'Bad Refugees': A Conversation with Viet Thanh Nguyen," *Los Angeles Review of Books,* 24 September 18.

27. Hannah Arendt, "We Refugees," in *Altogether Elsewhere: Writers on Exile,* ed. Marc Robinson (Boston: Faber and Faber, 1994), 111.

28. Monique Truong, "Diasporic Vietnamese Artists Network: A Discussion among Writers," The People's Forum, New York, 23 March 2019.

29. Monique T. D. Truong, "The Emergence of Voices: Vietnamese American Literature, 1975–1990," *Amerasia Journal* 19.3 (1993): 40.

30. Ibid., 30.

31. Ibid., 32.

32. Marguerite Nguyen, in her essential *American Dreams: The Longue Durée of U.S. Literature and Empire,* argues that a close proximity between American people, culture, and institutions and Vietnam existed long before war and refuge. This proximity is unacknowledged in most critical studies, and therefore the presumed "sudden" introduction of Southeast Asians as refugees is a historical error that helps narrativize the "emergency" necessary for the United States to stand as the unencumbered and noble rescuers of this population. Further, building on the work of Janet Lipman, Nguyen argues that the refugee camps (or "relocation camps") in the United States did provide some cultural and linguistic training so that refugees were not completely out of place in their new surroundings. Nonetheless, as is evident in her research into the Vietnamese-language writing of Vo Phien, despite this longer cultural contact with the United States than what is usually acknowledged, Vietnamese Americans did not have the sufficient time, training, and audience to develop a significant number of English-language works during the first wave of refuge. See Marguerite Nguyen. *American Dreams: The* Longue Durée *of*

U.S. Literature and Empire (Philadelphia: Temple University Press, 2018), 120–136.

33. Nhi T. Lieu. *The American Dream in Vietnamese* (Minneapolis: University of Minnesota Press, 2011), 200–201.

34. Isabelle Thuy Pelaud, *This is All I Choose to Tell: History and Hybridity in Vietnamese American Literature* (Philadelphia: Temple University Press, 2011), 125.

35. Michele Janette, "Vietnamese American Literature," in *The Oxford Encyclopedia of Asian American Literature and Culture* (Oxford: Oxford University Press, 2020).

36. Cathy J. Schlund-Vials, "(Re)Collecting Vietnam: Vietnamization, Soldier Remorse, and Marvel Comics," in *Drawing New Color Lines: Transnational Asian American Graphic Narratives*, ed. Monica Chiu (Hong Kong: Hong Kong University Press, 2014), 191.

37. Viet Thanh Nguyen, "Introduction," in *The Displaced: Refugee Writers on Refugee Lives*, ed. Viet Thanh Nguyen (New York: Abrams, 2018), 11.

38. Ibid., 22.

39. Ibid.

40. Ibid., 16.

41. Ibid.

42. Vu Tran, "A Refugee Again," in *The Displaced: Refugee Writers on Refugee Lives*, 155.

43. Ibid., 152.

44. Ibid., 153.

45. Cathy J. Schlund-Vials, "The Subjects of 1975: Delineating the Necessity of Critical Refugee Studies." *MELUS: Multi-Ethnic Literature of the U.S.* 41.3 (2016): 202.

46. Yến Lê Espiritu, *Body Counts: The Vietnam War and Militarized Refuge(es)* (Oakland: University of California Press, 2014), 8–9.

47. Mimi Thi Nguyen, *The Gift of Freedom: War, Debt, and Other Refugee Passages* (Durham, NC: Duke University Press, 2012), 180.

Chapter 1

1. Liisa Malkki, "Speechless Emissaries: Refugees, Humanitarianism, and Dehistoricization," *Cultural Anthropology* 11.3 (1996): 385.

2. W.J.T. Mitchell, *Seeing through Race* (Cambridge, MA: Harvard University Press, 2012), 127.

3. Ibid., 127–128.

4. Maya Arulpragasam (M.I.A.), "Borders" (Santa Monica, CA: Interscope Records, 2016).

5. Leo Chavez's research has shown that "the mass image is used on 39 percent of [magazine] covers specifically on the topic of refugees, but only

10 percent of covers more generally." Leo Chavez, *Covering Immigration: Popular Images and the Politics of the Nation* (Berkeley: University of California Press, 2001), 70.

6. Malkki, "Speechless Emissaries," 387–388.

7. Ibid., 54.

8. Ibid., 69.

9. Of course, we need to consider that M.I.A.'s video will circulate most vibrantly to those with access to broadband technology and other expensive technological devices.

10. David Campbell, "The Myth of Compassion Fatigue," David-Campbell.org.

11. Jacques Rancière, "The Intolerable Image," in *The Emancipated Spectator* (New York: Verso, 2009), 97.

12. Brad Evans, "Facing the Intolerable," Los Angeles Review of Books, 11 November 2014.

13. Jacques Rancière, commentary on Jaar's installation "Theater of Images," in *Alfredo Jaar: La Politique Des Images* (Lausanne: jrp/ringier, 2008), 76.

14. Susan Sontag, *Regarding the Pain of Others* (New York: Farrar, Straus, and Giroux, 2013), 21.

15. John Berger, "Photographs of Agony," in *About Looking* (New York: Vintage, 1992), 43.

16. Ibid.

17. I am borrowing the term "out of time" from Johannes Fabian's *Time and the Other*, where anthropology is accused of "making its object" by putting the anthropologist in the "here and now" while relegating other cultures to "there and then." See Johannes Fabian, *Time and the Other: How Anthropology Makes Its Object* (New York: Columbia University Press, 2002).

18. Berger, "Photographs of Agony," 44.

19. Ibid.

20. Katy Fallon, "Three Years on from Alan Kurdi's Death and Life Is No Better for Child Refugees in Europe," *The Independent*, 2 September 2018.

21. Susan Sontag, *Regarding the Pain of Others* (New York: Farrar, Straus, and Giroux, 2013), 71 (my emphasis).

22. Nerissa Marie Balce, *Body Parts of Empire: Visual Abjection, Filipino Images, and the American Archive* (Ann Arbor: University of Michigan Press, 2016), 72.

23. Susie Linfield, *Cruel Radiance: Photography and Political Violence* (Chicago: University of Chicago Press, 2012), 30.

24. Tom Petty, "Refugee," on *Damn the Torpedoes* (MCA Records, 1980).

25. Edward W. Said and Jean Mohr, *After the Last Sky: Palestine Lives* (New York: Columbia University Press, 1998), 4.

26. Trinh T. Minh-ha, *Elsewhere, within Here: Immigration, Refugeeism and the Boundary Event* (New York: Routledge, 2010), 46.

27. Jocelyn Sakal Froese, "Colour in Thi Bui's *The Best We Could Do*," Women Write about Comics.

28. Thi Bui, *The Best We Could Do: An Illustrated Memoir* (New York: Abrams ComicArts, 2017), 209–210.

29. Ibid., 207.

30. Parts of this discussion of GB Tran's *Vietnamerica* are revised from my chapter "Picturing the Past: Drawing Together Vietnamese American Transnational History" in *Global Asian American Popular Cultures,* eds Shilpa Davé, LeiLane Nishime, and Tasha Oren, 257–279 (New York: New York University Press, 2016).

31. Derek Parker Eisner, "Forward: Reading in the Gutter," in *Multicultural Comics: From Zap to Blue Beetle,* ed. Frederick Luis Aldama (Austin: University of Texas Press, 2010), ix.

32. Caroline Kyungah Hong, "Disorienting the Vietnam War: GB Tran's *Vietnamerica* as Transnational and Transhistorical Graphic Memoir," *Asian American Literature: Discourse and Pedagogies* 5 (2014): 18.

33. Catherine H. Nguyen, in "Illustrating Diaspora: History and Memory in Vietnamese American and French Graphic Novels," explains how in *Vietnamerica* each story fragment refracts through another via Tran's use of parallelism and color coding, whereby "the third page depicts . . . GB seated between his father and mother on a commercial flight to Vietnam [where] the colors are not as saturated and pale in comparison to the deep reds and rich blacks of the previous pages. With the spread encompassing war and saturated colors on the left . . . there is a clear visual juxtaposition between leaving and returning, between war and tourism, and between past and present" (204). However, Tran manipulates these scenes so that their distinctiveness reinforces the continuity between each individual part of story, with Nguyen offering that "the two scenes are clearly opposite yet very reminiscent of each other . . . both are tied together through GB and the notion of the journey" (204). This family history, then, is enhanced by contradictions and the multiplicity of perspectives, creating a dynamic and sensorially rich journey for the reader. See Catherine H. Nguyen, "Illustrating Diaspora: History and Memory in Vietnamese American and French Graphic Novels," in *Redrawing the Historical Past: History, Memory, and Multiethnic Graphic Novels,* ed. Martha Cutter and Cathy J. Schlund-Vials, 182–216 (Athens: University of Georgia Press, 2018).

34. Yến Lê Espiritu, "About Ghost Stories: The Vietnam War and 'Rememoration,'" *PMLA,* 123.5 (2008): 1700–1702.

35. Thu-hương Nguyễn-võ, "Forking Paths: How Shall We Mourn the Dead?," *Amerasia Journal* 31.2 (2005): 183.

36. Kandice Chuh, *The Difference Aesthetics Makes: On the Humanities "after Man"* (Durham, NC: Duke University Press, 2019), xii.

37. Sara Ahmed, *Strange Encounters: Embodied Others in Post-Coloniality* (New York: Routledge, 2000), 3.

38. Peter I. Rose, "Tempest-Tost: Exile, Ethnicity, and the Politics of Rescue," *Sociological Forum* 8.1 (1993): 6.

39. Ibid.

40. Stuart Hall, *Race: The Floating Signifier,* video, ed. Sut Jhally, Media Education Foundation, 1997.

41. W.J.T. Mitchell, *Seeing through Race* (Cambridge, MA: Harvard University Press, 2012), 4.

42. Ibid., 10.

Chapter 2

1. This chapter revises one of my earlier published pieces. See Timothy K. August, "Re-Placing the Accent: From the Exile to Refugee Position," *MELUS: Multi-Ethnic Literatures of the U.S.* 41.3 (2016): 68–88.

2. Vinh Nguyen, "Refugeetude: When Does a Refugee Stop Being a Refugee?," *Social Text* 37.2 (2019): 110.

3. Ibid.

4. As I explore in both the introduction and the conclusion of this book, when the writing coming from the refugee position is aestheticized, over time a style of refugee writing emerges. This style of writing is usable by both refugee and nonrefugee artists alike, whereby the refugee figure—or the negative experiences of refuge that Vinh Nguyen speaks of—can become a point of departure for a variety of stories and narratives.

5. This distinction between "identity" and "subjectivity" follows Christopher Lee's discussion of these two terms in his major work *The Semblance of Identity*. See Christopher Lee, *The Semblance of Identity: Aesthetic Mediation in Asian American Literature* (Stanford, CA: Stanford University Press, 2012), 2–3.

6. I wish to take a moment to acknowledge the labor that Southeast Asian American studies is currently performing to try remedying this disconnect. In particular, I would like to draw attention to Yến Lê Espiritu's *Body Counts* and her "critical refugee studies" work; the summer 2012 Southeast Asian American studies special issue of *positions*, edited by Mimi Thi Nguyen, Fiona I. B. Ngô, and Mariam B. Lam; and the fall 2015 special issue the *Asian American Literary Review* titled *(Re)Collecting the Vietnam War* and edited by Cathy J. Schlund-Vials and Sylvia Shin Huey Chong.

7. Edward Said, *Culture and Imperialism* (New York: Knopf, 1993), xxvi.

8. Edward Said, "Reflections on Exile," in *Reflections on Exile and Other Essays* (Cambridge, MA: Harvard University Press, 2000), 385; Robert Spencer, "'Contented Homeland Peace': The Motif of Exile in Edward

Said," in *Edward Said: A Legacy of Emancipation,* ed. Adel Iskandar and Hakem Rustom (Berkeley: University of California Press, 2010), 389.

9. Edward Said, *Culture and Imperialism* (New York: Knopf, 1993), xxvii.

10. Timothy Brennan, "The Critic and the Public: Edward Said and World Literature," in *Edward Said: A Legacy of Emancipation,* ed. Adel Iskandar and Hakem Rustom (Berkeley: University of California Press, 2010), 105.

11. Said, *Culture and Imperialism,* 336.

12. This is not to suggest that Said was in any way hostile or did not care about refugee communities. Rather, it is clear in his work that he had difficulty engaging with and representing the perils of the common Palestinian refugee experience when his own early refuge paled in comparison. Indeed, Said is conscious of this comparative problem and grapples with his own relative privilege throughout much of his work, understanding that while serving as the Parr Professor of English and Comparative Literature at Columbia University he was far removed from intimate problems and concerns of everyday Palestinian people. Interestingly, one of his responses to this dilemma was to turn to an aesthetic critique, commenting on the discursive and artistic forms that have been used to represent the Palestinian community at large. This approach is seen most directly in his 1986 collaboration with Jean Mohr, *After the Last Sky: Palestinian Lives* (New York: Columbia University Press, 1998).

13. Michele Janette, "Vietnamese American Literature in English 1963–1994," *Amerasia Journal* 29.1 (2003): 271–272.

14. Monique T. D. Truong, "The Emergence of Voices: Vietnamese American Literature, 1975–1990," *Amerasia Journal* 19.3 (1993): 30.

15. "On Sông I Sing: A Conversation between Bao Phi and Jane Kim," Coffeehousepress.org, Coffee House, 2011, para. 6.

16. Ibid., para. 24.

17. Phi acknowledges his debt to Sandra Cisneros in this piece, as underneath the title he notes that "You Bring Out the Vietnamese in Me" is inspired by Cisneros' poem "You Bring Out the Mexican in Me."

18. Bao Phi, excerpts from "You Bring Out the Vietnamese in Me" from *Sông I Sing.* Copyright © 2011 by Bao Phi. Reprinted with the permission of The Permissions Company, LLC on behalf of Coffee House Press, www.coffeehousepress.org.

19. Saymoukda Duangphouxay Vongsay, "When Everything Was Everything," *2012 Saint Paul Almanac,* ed. Duanell (Nam) Barnwell, Maya Beecham, Mary Davini, et al. (Saint Paul, MN: Arcata, 2012), 1–4. Used by permission of Saymoukda Vongsay.

20. Ibid., 18–23.

21. Ibid., 5–6.

22. Ibid., 16–17.

23. Saymoukda Duangphouxay Vongsay, *Saymoukda Duangphouxay Vongsay: Immigrant Stories,* YouTube, 24 February 2015, https://www.youtube.com/watch?v=cW9-zwU7_2I.

24. Yến Lê Espiritu "Toward a Critical Refugee Studies: The Vietnamese Refugee Subject in US Scholarship," *Journal of Vietnamese Studies* 1.1–2 (2006): 410–411.

25. Ibid., 421.

26. Giorgio Agamben. *Means without End: Notes on Politics,* trans. Vincenzo Binetti and Cesare Casarino (Minneapolis: University of Minnesota Press, 2000), 16.

27. Viet Thanh Nguyen, "Refugee Memories and Asian American Critique," *positions* 20.3 (2012): 928–930.

28. Ibid., 923–925.

29. Ibid., 931. The discussion of a rooted versus postnational position mirrors the earlier debates in Asian American studies explored in Sau-ling C. Wong's seminal essay "Denationalization Reconsidered: Asian American Cultural Criticism at a Crossroads," in *Postcolonial Theory and the United States: Race, Ethnicity, and Literature,* ed. Amritjit Singh and Peter Schmidt, 122–149 (Jackson: University of Mississippi Press, 2000). Wong critiques the emergence of what she sees as a "developmental model" where domestic Asian American concerns end up advancing to a new "stage" of transnational concerns—preferring instead the language of "modes" or "phases," where the location of Asian American subjectivity extends or contracts depending on the historical moment at hand (138). She is wary of the uneven privileges accorded to those who identify transnationally, noting that "class bias is coded into the privileging of travel and transnational mobility" (136). Indeed, in a note of caution she urges those writing on Asian American cultural criticism to reconsider the foundations provided by the horizontal comradeships developed in a nation-state, as at times these bonds can contextualize, historicize, and politicize a community's experiences in a more material and practical manner than transnational ties can (135–136, 139).

30. Nguyen's argument in "Refugee Memories and Asian American Critique" goes on to claim that Hmong literature's desire for national belonging necessarily ends up inviting an American readership that judges Hmong work through the limiting standards of "minority" or "ethnic" literature. While Nguyen's piece—and indeed the body of his scholarship—is essential reading that moves the field of Southeast Asian American studies forward, in this chapter I am identifying a creative reenvisioning of the refugee position that anticipates this partitioning of ethnic experience. With this new expansion of the refugee position, the refugee is not merely a subaltern voice that cannot be heard; rather, aestheticizing the refugee position is a way of remembering, honoring, and representing what Yến Lê Espiritu calls the "ongoingness" of war and refugee life (22). My claim problematizes his

assertion that "As for the refugee who speaks in a language that her adopted national audience can hear, her dilemma is that she has ceased being a refugee even as she speaks in the refugee's name" (933).

31. For further discussion of the conditions of the proletariat's class consciousness, see "The Standpoint of the Proletariat" in Georg Lúkacs, *History and Class Consciousness: Studies in Marxist Dialectics,* 149–222 (Cambridge, MA: MIT Press, 1972).

32. Benedict Anderson, "The Unrewarded: Notes on the Nobel Prize for Literature," *New Left Review* 80 (2013): 104.

33. Andrew Lam, *Perfume Dreams: Reflections on the Vietnamese Diaspora* (Berkeley CA: Heyday, 2005), 19.

34. Ibid., 22.

35. Andrew Lam, *East Eats West: Writing in Two Hemispheres* (Berkeley, CA: Heyday, 2010), 130.

36. Kao Kalia Yang, *The Late Homecomer: A Memoir* (Minneapolis: Coffee House, 2008), 4.

37. Kao Kalia Yang, "To See a Bigger World: The Home and Heart of a Hmong American Writer," in *Hmong and American: From Refugees to Citizens,* ed. Vincent K. Her and Mary Louise Buley-Meissner (Saint Paul: Minnesota Historical Press, 2012), 225.

38. Ibid., 227.

39. Ibid., 226.

40. Ibid., 231.

41. Mai Neng Moua, ed., *Bamboo among the Oaks: Contemporary Writing by Hmong Americans* (Saint Paul, MN: Borea Books, 2002), 3.

42. Bao Phi, "You Bring Out the Vietnamese in Me," in *Sông I Sing* (Minneapolis: Coffee House, 2011), 18–19.

43. Agnes Heller, *Aesthetics and Modernity: Essays by Agnes Heller,* ed. John Rundell, (New York: Lexington Books, 2011), 19.

44. Edward Said, "Intellectual Exile: Expatriates and Marginals." *Grand Street* 47.3 (1993): 119.

45. Edward Said, "Reflections on Exile," in *Reflections on Exile and Other Essays* (Cambridge, MA: Harvard University Press, 2000), 181.

46. Trinh T. Minh-ha, *Elsewhere, within Here: Immigration, Refugeeism and the Boundary Event* (New York: Routledge, 2010), 150.

Chapter 3

1. Aimee Phan, *The Reeducation of Cherry Truong* (New York: St. Martin's, 2012), 5.

2. Evyn Lê Espiritu, "Vexed Solidarities: Vietnamese Israelis and the Question of Palestine," *LIT: Literature, Interpretation, Theory* 29.1 (2018): 8–28.

3. Quynh Nhu Le, "The Colonial Choreographies of Refugee Resettlement in Lan Cao's Monkey Bridge," *Journal of Asian American Studies* 21.3 (2018): 398.

4. Robert Tally Jr., *Spatiality* (New York: Routledge, 2013), 28.

5. Tina Y. Chen, "Emergent Cartographies and the Directions of Asian American Literary Studies," *American Literary History* 23.4 (2011): 885.

6. Viet Thanh Nguyen, "March Book Club Pick: *Exit West,* by Mohsin Hamid." *New York Times,* 10 March 2017.

7. Mohsin Hamid, *Exit West* (New York: Penguin, 2017), 1.

8. Ibid., 23.

9. Ibid.

10. Nguyen, "March Book Club Pick."

11. Mohsin, *Exit West,* 94.

12. Ibid., 100.

13. Ibid., 101.

14. Ibid., 120.

15. Ibid., 126.

16. Ibid.

17. Edward Said, *Culture and Imperialism* (New York: Knopf, 1993), 7.

18. Fredric Jameson, "Cognitive Mapping," in *Marxism and the Interpretation of Culture,* ed. Cary Nelson and Lawrence Grossberg (Urbana-Champaign: University of Illinois Press, 1988), 350.

19. Sau-Ling Wong, *Reading Asian American Literature: From Necessity to Extravagance* (Princeton, NJ: Princeton University Press, 1993), 133.

20. Ibid., 134.

21. William Boelhower, *Through a Glass Darkly: Ethnic Semiosis in American Literature* (New York: Oxford University Press, 1987), 49.

22. Yến Lê Espiritu and Lan Duong. "Feminist Epistemology: Reading Displacement in Vietnamese and Syrian Refugee Art," *Signs: Journal of Women in Culture and Society* 43.3 (2018): 606.

23. Ibid., 588.

24. Robert Tally Jr., *The Geocritical Legacies of Edward W. Said* (New York: Palgrave Macmillan, 2015), 4.

25. Franco Moretti, *Graphs, Maps, Trees: Abstract Models for Literary History* (New York: Verso, 2007), 55.

26. Phan, *The Reeducation of Cherry Truong,* 23.

27. Seth Mydens, "Ho Chi Minh City Hurries to Become a Megacity," *New York Times,* 17 November 2006.

28. Phan, *The Reeducation of Cherry Truong,* 3.

29. Long Bui, "The Debts of Memory: Historical Amnesia and Refugee Knowledge in The Reeducation of Cherry Truong," *Journal of Asian American Studies* 18.1 (2015): 82–83.

30. Phan, *The Reeducation of Cherry Truong,* 347–349.

31. Kandice Chuh, *Imagine Otherwise: On Asian Americanist Critique* (Durham, NC: Duke University Press, 2003), 86.
32. Ibid., 86–87.
33. Phan, *The Reeducation of Cherry Truong*, 18–19.
34. Personal communication. Following Rei Magosaki's insightful respondent comments at the 2018 American Studies Association conference in Atlanta, Georgia, over text I asked Aimee Phan if "Newport Lake" was indeed an amalgamation of Newport Beach and Lake Forest.

Chapter 4

1. Nguyen has also been appointed the Aerol Arnold Chair of English and a University Professor at the University of Southern California.
2. Viet Thanh Nguyen, *Race and Resistance: Literature and Politics in Asian American America* (New York: Oxford University Press, 2002), 3.
3. Ibid., vi.
4. Angela Chen, "Pulitzer Winner Viet Thanh Nguyen: 'My Book Has Something to Offend Everyone,'" *The Guardian,* 22 April 2016.
5. Edward Said, "The Public Role of Writers and Intellectuals," in *The Public Intellectual,* ed. Helen Small (Oxford, UK: Blackwell, 2002), 36–39.
6. David K. Shipler, "A Child's Tour of Duty," Review of *When Heaven and Earth Changed Places* by Le Ly Hayslip, *New York Review of Books,* 25 June 1989.
7. It is also worth noting the genders of the authors involved. Going back to the Maxine Hong Kingston-Frank Chin controversy, Asian American women's writing has been slandered by some critics as providing less than authentic and/or accurate accounts of the Asian American experience. While the hope is that this chauvinistic critique is not given much credence in the present day, one could surmise that Nguyen's work benefits from a critical structural hangover, considering the large disparity in visibility accorded to him versus other Vietnamese American writers.
8. Betsy Huang, *Contesting Genre in Contemporary Asian American Fiction* (New York: Palgrave Macmillan, 2010), 1.
9. Kathryn Cope, *The Sympathizer: A Guide for Book Clubs* (n.p.: CreateSpace, 2016), 45.
10. Daniel Kim made this observation during the roundtable titled "Give and Take: Reading *The Sympathizer* together" at the Association for Asian American Studies national conference on 13 April 2017.
11. This postcolonial operation, where cultural knowledge is created to justify military intervention, is most famously and thoroughly described in Edward Said, *Culture and Imperialism* (New York: Knopf, 1993), xi–14.
12. Karl Ashoka Britto. "The Stranger's Choice," Review of *The Sympathizer* by Viet Thanh Nguyen, *Public Books,* 1 August 2015.
13. Nguyen, *Race and Resistance,* 7.

14. Viet Thanh Nguyen, "Speak of the Dead, Speak of Viet Nam: The Ethics and Aesthetics of Minority Discourse," *CR: The New Centennial Review* 6.2 (2006): 9.

15. Ibid., 10.

16. Nguyen published his novel *The Sympathizer* in 2015, his academic treatise *Nothing Ever Dies: Vietnam and the Memory of War* in 2016, and his collection of short stories, *The Refugees*, in 2017.

17. Sarah Brouillette, *Postcolonial Writers in the Global Literary Marketplace* (New York: Palgrave McMillan, 2007), 2.

18. Viet Thanh Nguyen, "What Is Vietnamese American Literature?," in *Looking Back on the Vietnam War: Twenty-First Century Perspectives*, ed. Brenda M. Boyle and Jeehyun Lim (New Brunswick, NJ: Rutgers University Press), 54.

19. Ibid., 50.

20. Ibid., 53.

21. Ibid., 55.

22. Ibid., 53.

23. Ibid., 61.

24. See Yến Lê Espiritu, *Body Counts: The Vietnam War and Militarized Refuge(es)* (Oakland: University of California Press, 2014), and Mimi Thi Nguyen, *The Gift of Freedom: War, Debt, and Other Refugee Passages* (Durham, NC: Duke University Press, 2012).

25. Terry Gross, "Author Viet Thanh Nguyen Discusses 'The Sympathizer' and His Escape from Vietnam," Fresh Air, 17 May 2015.

26. For instance, many Vietnamese refugees to the United States were also migrants in 1955 when Vietnam was split into the North and the South due to a colonial divide.

27. Viet Thanh Nguyen, *Nothing Ever Dies: Vietnam and the Memory of War* (Cambridge, MA: Harvard University Press, 2016), 248.

28. Arundhati Roy, "The 2004 Sydney Peace Prize Lecture," Seymour Theatre Centre, University of Sydney, Sydney Australia, 4 November 2004.

29. Susan Koshy, "The Rise of the Asian American Novel," in *The Cambridge History of the American Novel*, ed. Leonard Cassuto, Clare Virginia Bay, and Benjamin Reiss (New York: Cambridge University Press, 2011), 1059.

30. Ibid.

31. Tina Chen, *Double Agency: Acts of Impersonation in Asian American Literature and Culture* (Palo Alto, CA: Stanford University Press, 2005), xviii.

32. Rachel Ng, "Pulitzer Prize Winner Reflects on Misconceptions about Refugees," USC Trojan Family, Autumn 2016.

33. This is a reoccurring theme of Viet Thanh Nguyen's *Nothing Ever Dies: Vietnam and the Memory of War* (Cambridge, MA: Harvard University Press, 2016).

34. Nguyen, *The Sympathizer* (New York: Grove, 2015), 107.

35. Ricardo Herrera Bandrich, "The Vietnam War, the American War," interview with Viet Thanh Nguyen, Los Angeles Review of Books, 9 April 2016.

36. David Seed, "Spy Fiction." in *The Cambridge Companion to Crime Fiction,* ed. Martin Priestman (New York: Cambridge University Press, 2003), 115.

37. I am borrowing the notion of the importance in reading the narrator as a literal "bastard" from a more complex idea that has been fleshed out in a paper produced by Stony Brook University Ph.D. student Hyosun Lee.

38. Nguyen, *The Sympathizer,* 1.

39. Tina Chen, "Impersonation and Other Disappearing Acts in *Native Speaker* by Chang-Rae Lee," *Modern Fiction Studies,* 48.3 (2002): 638.

40. Ibid., 640.

41. Tavis Smiley, "Professor and Author Viet Thanh Nguyen," *The Tavis Smiley Show,* 7 April 2016.

42. Kerri Miller, "Viet Thanh Nguyen on Hiding in Plain Sight," *MPR News,* 9 May 2016.

43. Ibid.

44. Marguerite Nguyen and Catherine Fung, eds., *Refugee Cultures: Forty Years after the Vietnam War,* special issue of *MELUS: Multi-Ethnic Literature of the United States* 41.3 (2016): 2.

45. Nguyen, *The Sympathizer,* 3.

46. Jessica Gelt, "Viet Thanh Nguyen Tackles the War's Afterlife in *The Sympathizer*," *Los Angeles Times,* 10 June 2015.

47. Ibid.

48. Betsy Huang, *Contesting Genre in Contemporary Asian American Fiction* (New York: Palgrave Macmillan, 2010), 1.

49. Miller, "Viet Thanh Nguyen on Hiding in Plain Sight."

Conclusion

1. Laura Moss, Brendan McCormack, and Lucia Lorenzi, "On Refugees, Running and the Politics of Writing," *Canadian Literature* 232 (2017): 15.

2. Since Mohsin Hamid is also not a refugee, his aforementioned *Exit West* could be said to provide a similarly comforting narrative for the *New Yorker* crowd.

3. When promoting his installations about the refugee condition, Ai Weiwei claims that he empathizes with the struggles of those seeking asylum because he himself was a "child refugee," as his family was sentenced to labor camps in China. That said, his position cannot be considered an exact match with those who have endured refuge as it is legally defined. He would more properly be considered an internally displaced person, which means that while perhaps empathetic in an important and insightful manner, his

aesthetic approach would not share the same testimonial narrative influence that, I argue, is experienced by those once legally designated as refugees.

4. Thomas O. Haakensen, "The Refugee Affect: Ai Weiwei in Berlin," *EuropeNow* 4 April 2019.

5. Ai Weiwei, "*The Law of the Journey*: Exhibition Material," *Biennale of Sydney,* 28 May 2018.

6. Ai Weiwei, "The Refugee Crisis Isn't about Refugees, It's about Us," *The Guardian,* 2 February 2018.

7. For a discussion of the untrustworthy narrator, Bình, see the introduction to this volume.

8. Monica Sok, "The Cambodian American Writers Who Are Reimagining Cambodian American Literature: 5 Writers Discuss Subverting Conventions and Writing against the Trauma Narrative," Electric Lit, 11 June 2019.

9. Ibid.

10. Ibid.

11. Ibid.

12. Cathy J. Schlund-Vials, *War, Genocide, and Justice: Cambodian American Memory Work* (Minneapolis: University of Minnesota Press, 2012), 184.

13. Stuart Hall, *Race: The Floating Signifier,* ed. Sut Jhally (Video, Media Education Foundation, 1997).

14. The idea of a refugee critical consciousness builds on the insights of Keya Ganguly's "Exile as a Political Aesthetic," in *After Said: Postcolonial Literary Studies in the Twenty-First Century,* ed. Bahir Abu-Manneh, 69–86 (Cambridge: Cambridge University Press, 2019).

15. The Diasporic Vietnamese American Artist Network is led by scholar/artists Viet Thanh Nguyen and Isabelle Thuy Pelaud.

16. The Critical Studies Collective is a University of California initiative headed by scholars Lan Duong and Yến Lê Espiritu.

Bibliography

Adorno, Theodor. *Minima Moralia: Reflections from Damaged Life.* Trans. E.F.N. Jephcott. New York: Verso, 2006.
Agamben, Giorgio. *Homo Sacer: Sovereign Power and Bare Life.* Trans. Daniel Heller-Roazen. Palo Alto, CA: Stanford University Press, 1998.
———. *Means without End: Notes on Politics.* Trans. Vincenzo Binetti and Cesare Casarino. Minneapolis: University of Minnesota Press, 2000.
Ahmed, Sara. *Strange Encounters: Embodied Others in Post-Coloniality.* New York: Routledge, 2000.
Anderson, Benedict. "The Unrewarded: Notes on the Nobel Prize for Literature." *New Left Review* 80 (2013): 99–108.
Apter, Emily. "Global *Translatio*: The 'Invention' of Comparative Literature, Istanbul, 1933." In *Debating World Literature,* ed. Christopher Prendergast, 76–109. London: Verso, 2004.
Arendt, Hannah. "We Refugees." In *Altogether Elsewhere: Writers on Exile,* ed. Marc Robinson. Boston: Faber and Faber, 1994.
Arulpragasam, Maya [M.I.A.]. "Borders." Santa Monica, CA: Interscope Records, 2016.
Ashcroft, Bill. "Towards a Postcolonial Aesthetics." *Journal of Postcolonial Writing* 51.4 (2015): 410–421.
Ashcroft, Bill, Gareth Griffiths, and Helen Tiffin. *The Empire Writes Back: Theory and Practice in Post-Colonial Literatures.* New York: Routledge, 1989.

August, Timothy K. "Displaced Subjects and Refugee Literature." *Asian American Literature in Transition, 1965–1996*. Cambridge: Cambridge University Press, forthcoming.
Azoulay, Arielle. *The Civil Contract of Photography*. Cambridge, MA: MIT Press, 2012.
Bakhtin, Mikhail. *Art and Answerability: Early Philosophical Essays by M. M. Bakhtin*. Ed. Michael Holquist and Vladimir Liapunov. Austin: University of Texas Press, 1990.
Balce, Nerissa Marie. *Body Parts of Empire: Visual Abjection, Filipino Images, and the American Archive*. Ann Arbor: University of Michigan Press, 2016.
Bandrich, Ricardo Herrera. "The Vietnam War, the American War," Interview with Viet Thanh Nguyen, *Los Angeles Review of Books*, 9 April 2016. Web.
Bell, Susan. "Voices from Vietnam." USC Dornsife College News, 14 April 2015. Web.
Berger, John. "Photographs of Agony." In *About Looking*, 41–44. New York: Vintage, 1992.
Boelhower, William. *Through a Glass Darkly: Ethnic Semiosis in American Literature*. New York: Oxford University Press, 1987.
Brennan, Timothy. "The Critic and the Public: Edward Said and World Literature." In *Edward Said: A Legacy of Emancipation*, ed. Adel Iskandar and Hakem Rustom, 102–120. Berkeley: University of California Press, 2010.
Britto, Karl Ashoka. "The Stranger's Choice." Review of *The Sympathizer* by Viet Thanh Nguyen. *Public Books,* 1 August 2015. Web.
Brouillette, Sarah. *Postcolonial Writers in the Global Literary Marketplace*. New York: Palgrave McMillan, 2007.
Buckley, Christine. "'Good Refugees' and 'Bad Refugees': A Conversation with Viet Thanh Nguyen." *Los Angeles Review of Books,* 24 September 2018.
Bui, Long. "The Debts of Memory: Historical Amnesia and Refugee Knowledge in *The Reeducation of Cherry Truong*." *Journal of Asian American Studies* 18.1 (2015): 73–97.
Bui, Thi. *The Best We Could Do: An Illustrated Memoir*. New York: Abrams ComicArts, 2017.
Cabrera, Valarie. "An Act of Justice: An Interview with Viet Thanh Nguyen." The Writer's Block Blog, 30 Apr. 2015. Web.
Campbell, David. "The Myth of Compassion Fatigue." David-Campbell.org. Web.
Campomanes, Oscar V. "New Formations of Asian American Studies and U.S. Imperialism." *positions* 5.2 (1997): 523–550.
Cao, Lan. *Monkey Bridge: A Novel*. New York: Penguin, 1998.

Caputo, Phillip. "'The Sympathizer,' by Viet Thanh Nguyen." Book review of *The Sympathizer* by Viet Thanh Nguyen. *New York Times,* 2 April 2015. Web.
Cawelti, John G., and Bruce A. Rosenberg. *The Spy Story.* Chicago: University of Chicago Press, 1987.
Chan, Sucheng. *The Vietnamese American 1.5 Generation: Stories of War, Revolution, Flight, and New Beginnings.* Philadelphia: Temple University Press, 2006.
Chau, Angie. *Quiet as They Come.* Brooklyn, NY: Ig Publishing, 2010.
Chavez, Leo. *Covering Immigration: Popular Images and the Politics of the Nation.* Berkeley: University of California Press, 2001.
Chen, Angela. "Pulitzer Winner Viet Thanh Nguyen: 'My Book Has Something to Offend Everyone.'" *The Guardian,* 22 April 2016. Web.
Chen, Tina Y. *Double Agency: Acts of Impersonation in Asian American Literature and Culture.* Palo Alto, CA: Stanford University Press, 2005.
———. "Emergent Cartographies and the Directions of Asian American Literary Studies." *American Literary History* 23.4 (2011): 885–898.
———. "Impersonation and Other Disappearing Acts in *Native* Speaker by Chang-Rae Lee." *Modern Fiction Studies* 48.3 (2002): 637–667.
Ch'ien, Evelyn. "Interview with Viet Thanh Nguyen, Author of *The Sympathizer.*" *Hyphen: Asian America Unbridged,* 10 April 2015. Web.
Chuh, Kandice. *The Difference Aesthetics Makes: On The Humanities "After Man."* Durham, NC: Duke University Press, 2019.
———. *Imagine Otherwise: On Asian Americanist Critique.* Durham, NC: Duke University Press, 2003.
Cisneros, Sandra. *Loose Women: Poems.* New York: Vintage, 1994.
Clifford, James. *Routes: Travel and Translation in the Late Twentieth Century.* Cambridge, MA: Harvard University Press, 1997.
Cope, Kathryn. *The Sympathizer: A Guide for Book Clubs.* n.p.: CreateSpace, 2016.
Dinh, Linh. *Love Like Hate: A Novel.* New York: Seven Stories, 2010.
Eagleton, Terry. *The Ideology of the Aesthetic.* New York: Blackwell, 1991.
Elliot, Emory, Lou Freitas Caton, and Jeffrey Rhyne, eds. *Aesthetics in a Multicultural Age.* New York: Oxford University Press, 2002.
Espiritu, Yến Lê. "About Ghost Stories: The Vietnam War and 'Rememoration.'" *PMLA* 123.5 (2008): 1700–1702.
———. *Body Counts: The Vietnam War and Militarized Refuge(es).* Oakland: University of California Press, 2014.
———. "Toward a Critical Refugee Studies: The Vietnamese Refugee Subject in US Scholarship." *Journal of Vietnamese Studies* 1.1–2 (2006): 410–433.

Espiritu, Yến Lê, and Lan Duong. "Feminist Epistemology: Reading Displacement in Vietnamese and Syrian Refugee Art." *Signs: Journal of Women in Culture and Society* 43.3 (2018): 587–615.

Evans, Brad. "Facing the Intolerable." *Los Angeles Review of Books*, 11 November 2014. Web.

Fabian, Johannes. *Time and the Other: How Anthropology Makes Its Object*. New York: Columbia University Press, 2002.

Fallon, Katy. "Three Years on from Alan Kurdi's Death and Life Is No better for Child Refugees in Europe." *Independent*, 2 September 2018. Web.

Freeman, John. "Talking to Pulitzer Prize-Winning Author Viet Thanh Nguyen." Literary Hub, 18 April 2016. Web.

Froese, Jocelyn Sakal. "Colour in Thi Bui's *The Best We Could Do*." Women Write about Comics. Web.

Ganguly, Keya. "Exile as a Political Aesthetic." In *After Said: Postcolonial Literary Studies in the Twenty-First Century*, ed. Bahir Abu-Manneh, 69–86. Cambridge: Cambridge University Press, 2019.

Geetz, Clifford. *The Interpretation of Cultures*. New York: Basic Books, 1973.

Gelt, Jessica. "Viet Thanh Nguyen Tackles the War's Afterlife in *The Sympathizer*." *Los Angeles Times*, 10 June 2015. Web.

Gilbert, Sophie. "*Exit West* and the Edge of Dystopia." Book Review of *Exit West* by Moshin Hamid. *The Atlantic*, 8 Mar 2017. Web.

Gilroy, Paul. "The Black Atlantic as a Counterculture to Modernity." In *Theorizing Diaspora: A Reader*, ed. Jana Evans Braziel and Anita Mannur, 49–80. New York: Blackwell, 2003.

Gross, Terry. "Author Viet Thanh Nguyen Discusses 'The Sympathizer' and His Escape from Vietnam." Fresh Air, 17 May 2015. Web.

Haakenson, Thomas O. "The Refugee Affect: Ai Weiwei in Berlin." *EuropeNow*, 4 April 2019. Web.

Hall, Stuart. *Race: The Floating Signifier*. Ed. Sut Jhally. Video, Media Education Foundation, 1997.

Hamid, Mohsin. *Exit West*. New York: Penguin, 2017.

Hayslip, Le Ly. *When Heaven and Earth Changed Places: A Vietnamese Woman's Journey from War to Peace*. New York: Doubleday, 1989.

Heller, Agnes. *Aesthetics and Modernity: Essays by Agnes Heller*. Ed. John Rundell. New York: Lexington Books, 2011.

Hill, Lawrence. *The Illegal: A Novel*. New York: Norton, 2015.

Hong, Caroline Kyungah. "Disorienting the Vietnam War: GB Tran's *Vietnamerica* as Transnational and Transhistorical Graphic Memoir." *Asian American Literature: Discourse and Pedagogies* 5 (2014): 11–22.

Hsu, Madeline. "The Disappearance of America's Cold War Chinese Refugees, 1948–1966." *Journal of Ethnic American History* 31.4 (Summer 2012): 12–33.

Huang, Betsy. *Contesting Genre in Contemporary Asian American Fiction.* New York: Palgrave Macmillan, 2010.
Jameson, Fredric. "Cognitive Mapping." In *Marxism and the Interpretation of Culture,* ed. Cary Nelson and Lawrence Grossberg, 347–357. Urbana-Champaign: University of Illinois Press, 1988.
Janette, Michele. *My Viet: Vietnamese American Literature in English, 1962–Present.* Honolulu: University of Hawai'i Press, 2011.
———. "Vietnamese American Literature." In *The Oxford Encyclopedia of Asian American Literature and Culture,* ed. Josephine Lee. Oxford: Oxford University Press, 2020.
———. "Vietnamese American Literature in English 1963–1994." *Amerasia Journal* 29.1 (2003): 267–286.
Koshy, Susan. "The Rise of the Asian American Novel." In *The Cambridge History of the American Novel,* eds Leonard Cassuto, Clare Virginia Bay, and Benjamin Reiss, 1047–1063. New York: Cambridge University Press, 2011.
Kozol, Wendy. *Distant Wars Visible: The Ambivalence of Witnessing.* Minneapolis: University of Minnesota Press, 2014.
Lam, Andrew. *East Eats West: Writing in Two Hemispheres.* Berkeley, CA: Heyday, 2010.
———. *Perfume Dreams: Reflections on the Vietnamese Diaspora.* Berkeley, CA: Heyday, 2005.
Le, Quynh Nhu. "The Colonial Choreographies of Refugee Resettlement in Lan Cao's Monkey Bridge." *Journal of Asian American Studies* 21.3 (2018): 395–420.
Lee, Chang-Rae. *Native Speaker.* New York: Riverhead Books, 1995.
Lee, Christopher. "Diaspora, Transnationalism, and Asian American Studies: Positions and Debates." In *Displacements and Diasporas: Asians in the Americas,* ed. Wanni W. Anderson and Robert G. Lee, 23–38. New Brunswick, NJ: Rutgers University Press, 2005.
———. *The Semblance of Identity: Aesthetic Mediation in Asian American Literature.* Stanford, CA: Stanford University Press, 2012.
Lee, Erika. *The Making of Asian America: A History.* New York: Simon and Schuster, 2015.
Lee, Josephine. *Performing Asian America: Race and Ethnicity on the Contemporary Stage.* Philadelphia: Temple University Press, 1998.
Lee, Shelly Sang-Hee. *A New History of Asian America.* New York: Routledge, 2013.
Lê Espiritu, Evyn. "Vexed Solidarities: Vietnamese Israelis and the Question of Palestine." *LIT: Literature, Interpretation, Theory* 29.1 (2018): 8–28.
Lieu, Nhi T. *The American Dream in Vietnamese.* Minneapolis: University of Minnesota Press, 2011.
Lim, Shirley Geok-lin, and Cheng Lok Chua. *Tilting the Continent: Southeast Asian American Writing.* Minneapolis: New Rivers, 2000.

Linfield, Susie. *Cruel Radiance: Photography and Political Violence*. Chicago: University of Chicago Press, 2012.
Lukács, Georg. *History and Class Consciousness: Studies in Marxist Dialectics*. Cambridge, MA: MIT Press, 1972.
Lyall, Sarah. "'The Sympathizer: A Novel about a Soldier, Spy, and Film Consultant." Review of *The Sympathizer* by Viet Thanh Nguyen. *The New York Times*, 27 August 2015. Web.
Maeda, Daryl J. *Chains of Babylon: The Rise of Asian America*. Minneapolis: University of Minnesota Press, 2009.
Malkki, Liisa. "Refugees and Exile: From 'Refugee Studies' to the National Order of Things." *Annual Review of Anthropology* 24 (1995): 495–523.
———. "Speechless Emissaries: Refugees, Humanitarianism, and Dehistoricization." *Cultural Anthropology* 11.3 (1996): 377–404.
Manalansan, Martin, IV, Anita Mannur, and Robert Ji-Song Ku, eds. *Eating Asian America: A Food Studies Reader*. New York: New York University Press, 2013.
Miller, Kerri. "Viet Thanh Nguyen on Hiding in Plain Sight." MPR News, 9 May 2016. Web.
Mitchell, W.J.T. *Seeing through Race*. Cambridge, MA: Harvard University Press, 2012.
Moretti, Franco. *Graphs, Maps, Trees: Abstract Models for Literary History*. New York: Verso, 2007.
Moss, Laura, Brendan McCormack, and Lucia Lorenzi. "On Refugees, Running, and the Politics of Writing." *Canadian Literature* 232 (2017): 11–27.
Moua, Mai Neng, Ed. *Bamboo among the Oaks: Contemporary Writing by Hmong Americans*. Saint Paul, MN: Borea Books, 2002.
Mydans, Seth. "Ho Chi Minh City Hurries to Become a Megacity." *New York Times*, 17 November 2006. Web.
Ng, Rachel. "Pulitzer Prize Winner Reflects on Misconceptions about Refugees." *USC Trojan Family*, Autumn 2016. Web.
Ngô, Fiona, Mimi Thi Nguyen, and Mariam B. Lam. "Southeast Asian American Studies Special Issue: Guest Editors' Introduction." *Positions: East Asia Cultures Critique* 20.3 (2012): 671–684.
Nguyen, Bich Minh. *Stealing Buddha's Dinner: A Memoir*. New York: Penguin, 2008.
Nguyen, Catherine H. "Illustrating Diaspora: History and Memory in Vietnamese American and French Graphic Novels." In *Redrawing the Historical Past: History, Memory, and Multiethnic Graphic Novels*, ed. Martha Cutter and Cathy J. Schlund-Vials, 182–216. Athens: University of Georgia Press, 2018.
Nguyen, Marguerite. *America's Vietnam: The Longue Durée of U.S. Literature and Empire*. Philadelphia: Temple University Press, 2018.

Nguyen, Marguerite, and Catherine Fung, eds. *Refugee Cultures: Forty Years after the Vietnam War*, special issue of *MELUS: Multi-Ethnic Literature of the United States* 41.3 (2016).

Nguyen, Mimi Thi. *The Gift of Freedom: War, Debt, and Other Refugee Passages.* Durham, NC: Duke University Press, 2012.

Nguyen, Phuong Tran. *Becoming Refugee American: The Politics of Rescue in Little Saigon.* Champaign: University of Illinois Press, 2017.

Nguyen, Viet Thanh. "Introduction." In *The Displaced: Refugee Writers on Refugee Lives*, ed. Viet Thanh Nguyen. New York: Abrams, 2018.

———. "March Book Club Pick: 'Exit West,' by Mohsin Hamid." *New York Times*, 10 March 2017. Web.

———. *Nothing Ever Dies: Vietnam and the Memory of War.* Cambridge, MA: Harvard University Press, 2016.

———. *Race and Resistance: Literature and Politics in Asian American America.* New York: Oxford University Press, 2002.

———. "Refugee Memories and Asian American Critique." *positions* 20.3 (2012): 911–942.

———. "Speak of the Dead, Speak of Viet Nam: The Ethics and Aesthetics of Minority Discourse." *CR: The New Centennial Review* 6.2 (2006): 7–37.

———. *The Sympathizer.* New York: Grove, 2015.

———. "What Is Vietnamese American Literature?" In *Looking Back on the Vietnam War: Twenty-First Century Perspectives*, ed. Brenda M. Boyle and Jeehyun Lim, 50–63. New Brunswick, NJ: Rutgers University Press, 2016.

Nguyen, Vinh. "Refugeetude: When Does a Refugee Stop Being a Refugee?" *Social Text* 37.2 (2019): 109–131.

Nguyễn-võ, Thu-hương. "Forking Paths: How Shall We Mourn the Dead?" *Amerasia Journal* 31.2 (2005): 157–175.

Padilla, Genaro. "Interview with BA and PhD Alum Viet Thanh Nguyen." *The Wheeler Column: A UC Berkeley English Department Publication*, 11 September 2016. Web.

Palumbo-Liu, David. *The Deliverance of Others: Reading Literature in a Global Age.* Durham, NC: Duke University Press, 2012.

Pelaud, Isabelle Thuy. *This Is All I Choose to Tell: History and Hybridity in Vietnamese American Literature.* Philadelphia: Temple University Press, 2011.

Petty, Tom. "Refugee." *Damn the Torpedoes.* MCA Records, 1980.

Phan, Aimee. *The Reeducation of Cherry Truong.* New York: St. Martin's, 2012.

Phi, Bao. "On Sông I Sing: A Conversation between Bao Phi and Jane Kim." Coffeehousepress.org, 2011. Web.

———. "You Bring Out the Vietnamese in Me." In *Sông I Sing*, 9–12. Minneapolis: Coffee House, 2011.

Rancière, Jacques. "The Intolerable Image." *The Emancipated Spectator.* New York: Verso, 2009, 83–106.

Rose, Peter I. "Tempest-Tost: Exile, Ethnicity, and the Politics of Rescue." *Sociological Forum* 8.1 (1993): 5–24.

Roy, Arundhati. "The 2004 Sydney Peace Prize Lecture." Seymour Theatre Centre, University of Sydney, Australia, 4 November 2004. Web.

Said, Edward. *Culture and Imperialism.* New York: Knopf, 1993.

———. "Intellectual Exile: Expatriates and Marginals." *Grand Street* 47.3 (1993): 112–124.

———. "No Reconciliation Allowed." In *Letters of Transit,* ed. Andre Aciman, 87–114. New York: New Press, 1999.

———. "The Public Role of Writers and Intellectuals." In *The Public Intellectual,* ed. Helen Small, 19–39. Oxford, UK: Blackwell, 2002.

———. *Reflections on Exile and Other Essays.* Cambridge, MA: Harvard University Press, 2000.

Said, Edward W., and Jean Mohr. *After the Last Sky: Palestine Lives.* New York: Columbia University Press, 1998.

Schlund-Vials, Cathy J. "(Re)Collecting Vietnam: Vietnamization, Soldier Remorse, and Marvel Comics." In *Drawing New Color Lines: Transnational Asian American Graphic Narratives,* ed. Monica Chiu, 189–208. Hong Kong: Hong Kong University Press, 2014.

———. "The Subjects of 1975: Delineating the Necessity of Critical Refugee Studies." *MELUS: Multi-Ethnic Literature of the U.S.* 41.3 (2016): 199–203.

———. *War, Genocide, and Justice: Cambodian American Memory Work.* Minneapolis: University of Minnesota Press, 2012.

Schlund-Vials, Cathy J., and Sylvia Shin Huey Chong, eds. *(Re)Collecting the Vietnam War,* special issue of *Asian American Literary Review* 6.2 (2015).

SEARAC. "Data Disaggregation: What's the Problem with Current Education Data Collection and Reporting?" Fact Sheet, Washington, DC, February 2013. Web.

Seed, David. "Spy Fiction." In *The Cambridge Companion to Crime Fiction,* ed. Martin Priestman, 115–134. New York: Cambridge University Press, 2003.

Shemak, April. *Asylum Speakers: Caribbean Refugees and Testimonial Discourse.* New York: American Literatures Initiative, 2010.

Shipler, David K. "A Child's Tour of Duty." Review of *When Heaven and Earth Changed Places,* by Le Ly Hayslip. *New York Review of Books,* 25 June 1989. Web.

Smiley, Tavis. "Professor and Author Viet Thanh Nguyen." *The Tavis Smiley Show,* 7 April 2016.

Sok, Monica. "The Cambodian American Writers Who Are Reimagining Cambodian American Literature: 5 Writers Discuss Subverting

Conventions and Writing against the Trauma Narrative." Electric Lit, 11 June 2019. Web.

Song, Min Hyoung. "Asian American Literature within and beyond the Immigrant Narrative." In *Cambridge Companion to Asian American Literature,* ed. Crystal Parikh and Daniel Kim, 3–15. Cambridge: Cambridge University Press, 2015.

———. *The Children of 1965: On Writing, and Not Writing, as an Asian American.* Durham, NC: Duke University Press, 2013.

Sontag, Susan. *Regarding the Pain of Others.* New York: Farrar, Straus, and Giroux, 2013.

Spencer, Robert. "'Contented Homeland Peace': The Motif of Exile in Edward Said." In *Edward Said: A Legacy of Emancipation,* ed. Adel Iskandar and Hakem Rustom, 389–413. Berkeley: University of California Press, 2010.

Su, Lac. *I Love Yous Are for White People: A Memoir.* New York: HarperCollins, 2009.

Tally, Robert, Jr. *The Geocritical Legacies of Edward W. Said.* New York: Palgrave Macmillan, 2015.

———. *Spatiality.* New York: Routledge, 2013.

Tran, GB. *Vietnamerica: A Family's Journey.* New York: Villard, 2011.

Tran, Paul. "Viet Thanh Nguyen: Anger in the Asian American Novel." Asian American Writer's Workshop, 29 June 2015. Web.

Tran, Quan Tue. "Review of Body Counts: Militarized War and Militarized Refuge(es) by Yến Lê Espiritu." *Amerasia Journal* 41.1 (2015): 121–123.

Tran, Qui-Phiet. "Exiles in the Land of the Free: Vietnamese Artists and Writers in America, 1975 to the Present." *JASAT (Journal of the American Studies Association of Texas)* 20 (October 1989): 101–110.

Tran, Truong. *Placing the Accents.* Berkeley, CA: Apogee, 1999.

Tran, Vu. "A Refugee Again." In *The Displaced: Refugee Writers on Refugee Lives,* ed. Viet Thanh Nguyen, 151–158. New York: Abrams, 2018.

Trinh T. Minh-ha. *Elsewhere, within Here: Immigration, Refugeeism and the Boundary Event.* New York: Routledge, 2010.

Truong, Monique T. D. *The Book of Salt.* Boston: Mariner, 2003.

———. "The Emergence of Voices: Vietnamese American Literature, 1975–1990." *Amerasia Journal* 19.3 (1993): 27–50.

Võ, Linda Trinh. "The Vietnamese Experience: From Dispersion to the Development of Post-Refugee Communities." In *Asian American Studies: A Reader,* ed. Jean Yu-Wen Shen Wu and Min Song, 209–306. New Brunswick, NJ: Rutgers University Press, 2000.

Vongsay, Saymoukda Duangphouxay. "Saymoukda Duangphouxay Vongsay: Immigrant Stories." University of Minnesota Immigration History Center, 24 February 2015.

———. "When Everything Was Everything." In *2012 Saint Paul Almanac,* ed. Duanell (Nam) Barnwell, Maya Beecham, Mary Davini, et al., 22–23. Saint Paul, MN: Arcata, 2012.

Weiwei, Ai. *The Human Flow.* AC Films and Participant Media, Germany, 2017.

———. "*The Law of the Journey*: Exhibition Material." Biennale of Sydney, 28 May 2018. Web.

———. "The Refugee Crisis Isn't about Refugees, It's about Us." *The Guardian,* 2 February 2018. Web.

Wong, Sau-ling C. "Denationalization Reconsidered: Asian American Cultural Criticism at a Crossroads." In *Postcolonial Theory and the United States: Race, Ethnicity, and Literature,* ed. Amritjit Singh and Peter Schmidt, 122–149. Jackson: University of Mississippi Press, 2000.

———. *Reading Asian American Literature: From Necessity to Extravagance.* Princeton, NJ: Princeton University Press, 1993.

Wong, Yutian. *Choreographing Asian America.* Middletown, CT: Wesleyan University Press, 2010.

Yang, Gene Luen. *American Born Chinese.* New York: First Second, 2006.

Yang, Kao Kalia. *The Late Homecomer: A Memoir.* Minneapolis: Coffee House, 2008.

———. "To See a Bigger World: The Home and Heart of a Hmong American Writer." In *Hmong and American: From Refugees to Citizens,* ed. Vincent K. Her and Mary Louise Buley-Meissner, 225–232. Saint Paul: Minnesota Historical Press, 2012.

Yang, KaYing. "Southeast Asian American Children: Not the 'Model Minority.'" *Future of Children* 14.2 (2004): 127–133.

Zhou, Minh, and James V. Gatewood. *Contemporary Asian America: A Multidisciplinary Reader.* New York: New York University Press, 2000.

Index

Page numbers followed by the letter f refer to figures.

1.5-generation refugee writers, 19–20

Adams, Eddie, 39
Adorno, Theodor W., 9, 59, 75
aesthetics: aesthetic knowledge, 9–10; the aesthetic tradition, 8–15; and postcolonial literature, 8; refugee aesthetics, 12, 55–57, 125
After the Last Sky: Palestinian Lives (Said and Mohr), 37–38
Agamben, Giorgio, 67–68
agency, audience, and authority, 15–24
Ahmed, Sara, 51
Ai Weiwei, 127–128, 146n3
America Is in the Heart (S. Wong), 88
American Dreams: The Longue Durée of U.S. Literature and Empire (M. Nguyen), 135–136n32
Amusement dans la baraquement (Fun in the barracks [Hoang Quoc Bien]), 49–51, 50f
Anderson, Benedict, 51, 70
Arendt, Hannah, 15
artists, 68; Southeast Asian American, 13, 88, 132; Vietnamese American, 46–47

Asian America: Asian America and places of refuge, 81–87; future of, 94–97. *See also* refugee mapmaking
Asian American Literary Review (AALR), 131
Asian Americans, economic influence of in Asia, 91–92
Auerbach, Erich, 75
authors/writers, 125–126, 132, 139n4; Asian American women's writing, 144n7; Cambodian American, 129–130; Hmong American, 72–73, 73–74; and the literary marketplace, 102–112; non-Vietnamese American writing, 107; Southeast Asian American, 14, 56–57, 69–70, 103; Vietnamese, 103; Vietnamese American, 61–62, 71–72, 103, 107–108. *See also* spy novels, refugee

Bakhtin, Mikhail, 10
Balce, Nerissa Marie, 37
Bamboo among the Oaks: Contemporary Writing by Hmong Americans (Moua), 74

Berger, John, 35–36
Best We Could Do, The (Thi Bui), 39–41, 42f
Body Counts (Yen Lê Espiritu), 139n6
Book of Salt, The (Truong), 16, 100–101
"Borders" (M.I.A.), 27–28, 28–29f
Brennan, Timothy, 60
Bui, Thi, 39–40, 100
Bulosan, Carlos, 88–89

Cambodia/Cambodian Americans, 5, 45, 90, 130
Campbell, David, 32
Cao, Lan, 100
Carré, John le, 102
Chains of Babylon: The Rise of Asian America (Maeda), 81
Cham people/lands, 5
Chang, Henry, 112
Chau, Angie, 15
Chavez, Leo, 30, 136–137n5
Chen, Tina, 82, 112, 118–119
Choreographing Asian America (Y. Wong), 81
Chuh, Kandice, 10, 95
Chung, Tiffany, 89–90
Cold War, the, 5
Conrad, Joseph, 59
Contemporary Asian America (Zhou and Gatewood), 81
Cope, Kathryn, 102
Critical Refugee Studies Collective, 131

Dante, 58
Deliverance of Others, The: Reading in a Global Age (Palumbo-Liu), 116–117
"Denationalization Reconsidered: Asian American Cultural Criticism at a Crossroads" (S. L. Wong), 141n29
Diasporic Vietnamese American Artist Network (DVAN), 130–131
Dinh, Linh, 100, 111
"directionality of movement," 30
Double Agency (Chen), 112
Duong, Lan, 89

East Eats West (Lam), 70, 71
Eating Asian America (Manalansan, Mannur, and Ku), 81
Ellison, Ralph, 120
Espiritu, Yen Lê, 46, 66–67, 89, 108, 134n11, 139n6
ethnicity, of emblematic figures, 52
ethnocentrism, 58
exile position, 76; limits of, 57–62
Exit West (Hamid), 1, 80–81, 82–87

Fabian, Johannes, 137n17
Frankfurt School, 58

Gandhi, Evyn Lê Espiritu, 80
Gatewood, J. V., 81
George, Chris, 2
Gilbert, Sophie, 1–2
Gilroy, Paul, 134n12
Greene, Graham, 102
Gross, Terry, 103

Haakenson, Thomas O., 127
Hall, Stuart, 53, 130
Hamid, Mohsin, 1, 80–81, 82–87, 97, 128
Hayslip, Le Ly, 101
Heaven and Earth (1993), 101
Heller, Agnes, 75
Hill, Lawrence, 125–127, 128
Hirahara, Naomi, 112
Hmong/Hmong American people and lands, 5, 72–73
Hoang Quoc Bien, 49–51, 50f
Ho Chi Minh City, 91
Hollande, Francois, 36
Hong, Caroline Kyungah, 46
Hong Kong, 49, 50
Hsu, Madeline Y., 133n5
Hugo, Victor, 58
human face/refugee face distinction, 1–2

Illegal, The (Hill), 125–127
"Illustrating Diaspora: History and Memory in Vietnamese American and French Graphic Novels" (C. H. Nguyen), 138n33
"image-text," 27

immigrants: as refugees, 18–19; representation of, 52; Southeast Asian, 16–17
imperialism, capitalistic, 92
"infinityline," 30
Integrated Refugee & Immigrant Services (IRIS), 2–3
"Interviewer/respondent relationship," 62
Invisible Man, The (Ellison), 120
Iraq/Iraqis, 71, 73

Kim, Daniel, 102
Kozol, Wendy, 37
Ku, Robert Ji-Song, 81
Kurdi, Alan, 36

Lam, Andrew, 70–71, 76
Lam, Mariam, 5, 6
Lao/Lao American people and lands, 5
Late Homecomer, The (Yang), 72
Law of the Journey (Ai Weiwei), 127–128
Lawrence, D. H., 58
Lee, Chang Rae, 112, 117–118
Lee, Christopher, 9, 139n5
Lee, Don, 112
Lee, Erika, 81
Lee, Josephine, 81
Lee, Shelly Sang-Hee, 81
"Letter to a Young Iraqi Refugee to America" (Lam), 71
"Letter to a Young Refugee" (Lam), 70–71
Lieu, Nhi T., 17
Lin, Ed, 112
Linfield, Susie, 37
literary criticism, 75–76
literature: exile literature (*exilliteratur*), 58–59; German, 58; Hmong American, 73–74, 141n30; refugee, 68–69, 73–77; Southeast Asian, 16; Vietnamese American, 18, 47, 61–62, 106–107. *See also* authors/writers; spy novels, refugee
Little Saigons, 87–88, 90–91, 96–97; New Little Saigon, 79, 93
Lukács, George, 69

Maeda, Daryl, 81
Making of Asian America, The (E. Lee), 81
Malkki, Liisa, 13, 30
Manalansan, Martin, 81
Mannur, Anita, 81
memoirs, 61
Meyers, Seth, 103
M.I.A., 27–28, 32, 137n9
Miller, Kerri, 120
Mitchell, W.J.T., 27, 53
Mohr, Jean, 37
Moua, Mai Neng, 74
Mydan, Seth, 91

Native Speaker (C. Lee), 117–118
New History of Asian America, A (S. Lee), 81
Ngô, Fiona, 5
Nguyen, Bich Minh, 15, 69, 100
Nguyen, Catherine H., 138n33
Nguyen, Marguerite, 135–136n32
Nguyen, Mimi Thi, 5, 6, 67, 108
Nguyen Ngoc Loan, 39, 40
Nguyen, Phuong Tran 14, 20
Nguyen Tien Ngoc, 47, 48f, 49
Nguyen, Viet Thanh, 14–15, 18–19, 68, 69, 83, 98–100, 121–122, 124, 128; academic criticism of, 105–106; celebrity of, 99–100, 102–103; critical perspective of, 99; on Hmong literature, 141n30; and the "lost" Vietnamese version of the Vietnam War, 110–111; media appearances of, 122–123; professorial record and persona of, 99–100; as a refugee, 109; take of on the spy novel, 101–102, 112–120; on Vietnamese American authors, 107–108
Nguyen, Vinh, 56, 57
Nguyen-võ, Thu-huong, 46
Nothing Ever Dies: Vietnam and the Memory of War (Viet Thanh Nguyen), 105

Palumbo-Liu, David, 116–117
Pelaud, Isabelle Thuy, 17, 67
Performing Asian America (J. Lee), 81
Perfume Dreams (Lam), 70

Petty, Tom, 37
Phan, Aimee, 69, 78–81, 82, 88, 91, 94–95, 100
Phi, Bao, 62–64, 67, 69, 74–75, 76–77, 100

Quiet American, The (Greene), 102

Race and Resistance: Literature and Politics in Asian America (Viet Thanh Nguyen), 99, 104
racialization process, 53
racism, structural, 61–62
Rancière, Jacques, 32
Reeducation of Cherry Truong, The (Phan), 78–79, 82, 87, 90, 96–97; unsettled nature of the characters in, 92–94
refugee camps, 12–13
refugee images: 26–27, 33–37, 53–54, 136–137n5; as icons, 38, 39; as more than images of atrocity, 36–37; normalization of, 38–39; shock of, 36; symbolic play of, 54
refugee mapmaking, 87–94; "big data" maps that track refugee populations, 89–90; and the envisioning of blank spaces, 87; resonance of maps for the Vietnamese American community, 90; and state sovereignty, 87; supposed neutrality of maps, 90
"Refugee Memories and Asian American Critique" (Viet Thanh Nguyen), 141n30
refugees, 8–9; the "bad refugee," 98, 115, 129; centralizing of, 17–18; clandestinity and the refugee, 120–123; contemporary refugee life, 20–21; conventional representations of, 31–32; conventional rhetoric surrounding the refugee experience, 25–26; diversity of, 33; as an encroaching force, 30; formation of, 2; futures of, 124–132; heterogeneity of, 108–109; "good refugees," 14–15; as immigrants, 18–19; influence of rhetorical patterns on the reception of refugees, 2–3; Palestinian, 37–38; as perpetually foreign outsiders, 79–80; positioning of, 66–73, 76–77; refugee aesthetics, 12, 55–57; refugee communities, 54, 55; refugee encounters, 51–54; "refugee settler condition," 80; refugee subjectivity, 14–15, 59–60; and scholarly inquiry concerning (refugee studies), 57–58, 134n11; Southeast Asian, 6–7, 32, 34, 67, 68, 133n5; stateless refugees, 67–68; Syrian, 20, 32; tracking the presentation of, 11; as transformed into symbols of war, 34–35; uses and meanings concerning, 33–39; Vietnamese, 39–51; as watchers, 51. *See also* refugee images; refugee space
refugee space, 78–81, 94–97; Asian America and places of refuge, 81–87; division between refugee and settled space, 82–83; empty spaces, 90–91; as exceptional, 82; and the overcentralization of space, 82; relationship between physical orientation and ideas concerning space, 95; and the spatial expansion of "Vietnamese America," 91–92; tension between refugees and the space they inhabit, 94–95. *See also* refugee mapmaking
Rose, Charlie, 103
Rose, Peter, 52

Said, Edward, 37, 87, 100, 140n12; on exiles, 59–61; on the term "refugee," 75–76
Saigon Execution (Adams), 39–41
Schlund-Vials, Cathy J., 6
Seed, David, 115
Smiley, Tavis, 103
Smithsonian Asian Pacific American Center, 131
Sok, Monika, 129
Song, Min Hyoung 10
Sontag, Susan, 34, 36
"Southeast Asian America," 5–6
Southeast Asian American Studies Conference, 131
"Speak of the Dead, Speak of Vietnam: The Ethics and Aesthetics of

Minority Discourse" (Viet Thanh Nguyen), 104–105
Spencer, Robert, 59
Spitzer, Leo, 75
spy novels, refugee, 112–120; difference of from detective novels, 115–116
Sri Lankan Civil War (1983–2009), 27–28
Stone, Oliver, 101
Su, Lac,15
subjectivity: American, 141n29; claims of, 57; distinction between identity and subjectivity, 139n5; exile of, 60; inhabitable, 55; limits of, 112; new, 59; refugee, 14–15, 59–60
Svay, Sokunthary, 130
Sympathizer, The (Viet Thanh Nguyen), 98, 99, 102–103, 103–104, 106, 111–112; inhumanity represented by characters in, 113–114; promotion of, 121; as a refugee story, 109, 113–114; reviews of, 110; as simply an immigrant story, 108–109; as a spy novel, 113, 118–120; voice of, 128–129; as a work within the literary tradition of ethnic American fiction, 120–121

"Tempest-Tost: Exile, Ethnicity, and the Politics of Rescue" (Rose), 52
This is All I Choose to Tell (Pelaud), 17
Time and the Other (Fabian), 137n17
"To See a Bigger World: The Home and Heart of a Hmong American Writer" (Yang), 72
Tran, GB, 43–47, 100
Tran, Truong, 111
Tran, Vu, 111
Trinh Thi Minh Ha, 38
Truong, Monique, 16, 62, 100–101, 128

United Nations, 20
United Nations Convention Relating to the Status of Refugees (1951), 8–9, 134n15
Unreachable Trip (Nguyen Tien Ngoc), 47, 48f, 49
Unwanted Population, The (Chung), 89–90

Vang, Mai, 88
Vietnam War, 5, 31f, 39–51, 103, 104; American accounts of, 114
Vietnamerica: A Family's Journey (Tran), 43–46, 44f, 138nn30–31
Vietnamese boat people, 27, 29–30, 90
Voltaire, 58
Vongsay, Saymoukda Duangphoxay, 64–66, 67, 72, 76
Vuong, Ocean, 100

"We Refugees" (Arendt), 15
Westminster, California, 122
"What Is Vietnamese American Literature" (Viet Thanh Nguyen), 106–107
"When Everything Was Everything" (Vongsay), 64–66
When Heaven and Earth Changed Places: A Vietnamese Woman's Journey from War to Peace (Hayslip), 101
Wong, Sau-ling C., 10, 88, 141n29
Wong, Yutian, 81
Worra, Bryan Thao, 88

Yang, Kao Kalia, 72–73, 76
Yazeti, 73
"You Bring Out the Vietnamese in Me" (Bao Phi), 62–63, 74–75

Zhou, Minh, 81

Additional titles in this series:

Jiemin Bao, *Creating a Buddhist Community: A Thai Temple in Silicon Valley*
Elda E. Tsou, *Unquiet Tropes: Form, Race, and Asian American Literature*
Tarry Hum, *Making a Global Immigrant Neighborhood: Brooklyn's Sunset Park*
Ruth Mayer, *Serial Fu Manchu: The Chinese Supervillain and the Spread of Yellow Peril Ideology*
Karen Kuo, *East Is West and West Is East: Gender, Culture, and Interwar Encounters between Asia and America*
Kieu-Linh Caroline Valverde, *Transnationalizing Viet Nam: Community, Culture, and Politics in the Diaspora*
Lan P. Duong, *Treacherous Subjects: Gender, Culture, and Trans-Vietnamese Feminism*
Kristi Brian, *Reframing Transracial Adoption: Adopted Koreans, White Parents, and the Politics of Kinship*
Belinda Kong, *Tiananmen Fictions outside the Square: The Chinese Literary Diaspora and the Politics of Global Culture*
Bindi V. Shah, *Laotian Daughters: Working toward Community, Belonging, and Environmental Justice*
Cherstin M. Lyon, *Prisons and Patriots: Japanese American Wartime Citizenship, Civil Disobedience, and Historical Memory*
Shelley Sang-Hee Lee, *Claiming the Oriental Gateway: Prewar Seattle and Japanese America*
Isabelle Thuy Pelaud, *This Is All I Choose to Tell: History and Hybridity in Vietnamese American Literature*
Christian Collet and Pei-te Lien, eds., *The Transnational Politics of Asian Americans*
Min Zhou, *Contemporary Chinese America: Immigration, Ethnicity, and Community Transformation*
Kathleen S. Yep, *Outside the Paint: When Basketball Ruled at the Chinese Playground*
Benito M. Vergara Jr., *Pinoy Capital: The Filipino Nation in Daly City*
Jonathan Y. Okamura, *Ethnicity and Inequality in Hawai'i*
Sucheng Chan and Madeline Y. Hsu, eds., *Chinese Americans and the Politics of Race and Culture*
K. Scott Wong, *Americans First: Chinese Americans and the Second World War*
Lisa Yun, *The Coolie Speaks: Chinese Indentured Laborers and African Slaves in Cuba*
Estella Habal, *San Francisco's International Hotel: Mobilizing the Filipino American Community in the Anti-eviction Movement*

Thomas P. Kim, *The Racial Logic of Politics: Asian Americans and Party Competition*

Sucheng Chan, ed., *The Vietnamese American 1.5 Generation: Stories of War, Revolution, Flight, and New Beginnings*

Antonio T. Tiongson Jr., Edgardo V. Gutierrez, and Ricardo V. Gutierrez, eds., *Positively No Filipinos Allowed: Building Communities and Discourse*

Sucheng Chan, ed., *Chinese American Transnationalism: The Flow of People, Resources, and Ideas between China and America during the Exclusion Era*

Rajini Srikanth, *The World Next Door: South Asian American Literature and the Idea of America*

Keith Lawrence and Floyd Cheung, eds., *Recovered Legacies: Authority and Identity in Early Asian American Literature*

Linda Trinh Võ, *Mobilizing an Asian American Community*

Franklin S. Odo, *No Sword to Bury: Japanese Americans in Hawai'i during World War II*

Josephine Lee, Imogene L. Lim, and Yuko Matsukawa, eds., *Re/collecting Early Asian America: Essays in Cultural History*

Linda Trinh Võ and Rick Bonus, eds., *Contemporary Asian American Communities: Intersections and Divergences*

Sunaina Marr Maira, *Desis in the House: Indian American Youth Culture in New York City*

Teresa Williams-León and Cynthia Nakashima, eds., *The Sum of Our Parts: Mixed-Heritage Asian Americans*

Tung Pok Chin with Winifred C. Chin, *Paper Son: One Man's Story*

Amy Ling, ed., *Yellow Light: The Flowering of Asian American Arts*

Rick Bonus, *Locating Filipino Americans: Ethnicity and the Cultural Politics of Space*

Darrell Y. Hamamoto and Sandra Liu, eds., *Countervisions: Asian American Film Criticism*

Martin F. Manalansan IV, ed., *Cultural Compass: Ethnographic Explorations of Asian America*

Ko-lin Chin, *Smuggled Chinese: Clandestine Immigration to the United States*

Evelyn Hu-DeHart, ed., *Across the Pacific: Asian Americans and Globalization*

Soo-Young Chin, *Doing What Had to Be Done: The Life Narrative of Dora Yum Kim*

Robert G. Lee, *Orientals: Asian Americans in Popular Culture*

David L. Eng and Alice Y. Hom, eds., *Q & A: Queer in Asian America*

K. Scott Wong and Sucheng Chan, eds., *Claiming America: Constructing Chinese American Identities during the Exclusion Era*

Lavina Dhingra Shankar and Rajini Srikanth, eds., *A Part, Yet Apart: South Asians in Asian America*

Jere Takahashi, *Nisei/Sansei: Shifting Japanese American Identities and Politics*
Velina Hasu Houston, ed., *But Still, Like Air, I'll Rise: New Asian American Plays*
Josephine Lee, *Performing Asian America: Race and Ethnicity on the Contemporary Stage*
Deepika Bahri and Mary Vasudeva, eds., *Between the Lines: South Asians and Postcoloniality*
E. San Juan Jr., *The Philippine Temptation: Dialectics of Philippines–U.S. Literary Relations*
Carlos Bulosan and E. San Juan Jr., eds., *The Cry and the Dedication*
Carlos Bulosan and E. San Juan Jr., eds., *On Becoming Filipino: Selected Writings of Carlos Bulosan*
Vicente L. Rafael, ed., *Discrepant Histories: Translocal Essays on Filipino Cultures*
Yến Lê Espiritu, *Filipino American Lives*
Paul Ong, Edna Bonacich, and Lucie Cheng, eds., *The New Asian Immigration in Los Angeles and Global Restructuring*
Chris Friday, *Organizing Asian American Labor: The Pacific Coast Canned-Salmon Industry, 1870–1942*
Sucheng Chan, ed., *Hmong Means Free: Life in Laos and America*
Timothy P. Fong, *The First Suburban Chinatown: The Remaking of Monterey Park, California*
William Wei, *The Asian American Movement*
Yến Lê Espiritu, *Asian American Panethnicity*
Velina Hasu Houston, ed., *The Politics of Life*
Renqiu Yu, *To Save China, To Save Ourselves: The Chinese Hand Laundry Alliance of New York*
Shirley Geok-lin Lim and Amy Ling, eds., *Reading the Literatures of Asian America*
Karen Isaksen Leonard, *Making Ethnic Choices: California's Punjabi Mexican Americans*
Gary Y. Okihiro, *Cane Fires: The Anti-Japanese Movement in Hawaii, 1865–1945*
Sucheng Chan, *Entry Denied: Exclusion and the Chinese Community in America, 1882–1943*
Audrey Wu Clark, *The Asian American Avant-Garde: Universalist Aspirations in Modernist Literature and Art*
Eric Tang, *Unsettled: Cambodian Refugees in the New York City Hyperghetto*
Jeffrey Santa Ana, *Racial Feelings: Asian America in a Capitalist Culture of Emotion*

Timothy K. August is an Associate Professor of English at Stony Brook University.

www.ingramcontent.com/pod-product-compliance
Lightning Source LLC
Chambersburg PA
CBHW071847230426
43671CB00012B/2090